# SMETANA AND DVOŘÁK

# SYMPHONIA BOOKS
### A SERIES OF CONTRIBUTIONS TO THE HISTORY OF MUSIC

# SMETANA AND DVOŘÁK

THE CONTINENTAL BOOK COMPANY A. B., STOCKHOLM

# SMETANA
# AND DVOŘÁK

BY

## R. P. SUERMONDT

THE CONTINENTAL BOOK COMPANY A. B., STOCKHOLM

# INTRODUCTION

BY way of approaching the two Czech composers who form the subject of this short study, it is desirable to give a brief account of the musical development of their native land during the preceding centuries.

During the period of the Great Moravian Kingdom, 830–906, the influence of Byzantine civilization on the Czech and Slovakian countries was very considerable. And when the high level of musical accomplishment which had been reached in the centres of the Greek Empire is remembered, it can be safely assumed that Czech music profited in turn from this activity. In any case the words of the oldest known Czech hymn, "Gospodine, pomiluj ny" ("Lord, have mercy upon us"), follow the pattern set in the Greek Catholic liturgy, though whether the melody also antedates the eleventh century cannot be stated with certainty. This Song of Saint Adalbert, ascribed in legend to the Saint himself, belongs to-day to the living body of Czech culture.

After the fall of the Great Moravian Kingdom the Roman Catholic Church brought to the Czech and Slovakian lands music which had developed along other lines: namely Gregorian chant, the form into which the liturgical music of the earliest Christians had evolved. Subsequently Czech music took its orientation from the West, from Germany, France or Italy according to the varying degree of contact with those countries. These several streams of national, social and, above all, religious influence provided a strong impetus to the musical development of this very musically gifted people. They were able to fuse their native inheritance with external, foreign influences to create a quite individual art form.

During the period of the Moravian Principality, hymns for the church service were the most usual type of composition, secular songs following somewhat later. The religious plainsong, Gregorian chant, naturally flourished in the innumerable monasteries. Gradually Prague, which in

973 was made the seat of a bishopric, became the centre of this musical activity, which saw the composition of every possible variety of the Gregorian chorale, such as sequences, tropes, hymns and even choral dramatizations. The climax of this phase was reached during the thirteenth and fourteenth centuries. One of the most interesting chants of the period is "Svatý Václav", a hymn to Saint Wenceslaus, the national Patron Saint. The words and music of this late thirteenth-century composition have come down through the ages to reappear in "Variations on the old Bohemian Chorál Svatý Václav", originally for string quartet, later rewritten for string orchestra, by Josef Suk (1874–1935), best known abroad as a member of the Bohemian String Quartet, but at home regarded as one of the foremost composers of the last generation.

During that period when in Western Europe the ground prepared for polyphonic composition by the notations of such masters as Guillaume de Machaut and John Dunstable began to bear fruit in the works of Giles Binchois, Guillaume Dufay, Jan van Ockeghem and Jacobus Obrecht, the musicians of Bohemia remained faithful to plainsong, in which all the deepest emotions of the Czech people seemed to find expression. This was particularly the case after the appearance of Jan Hus and his disciples. The spiritual revolution when then took place inspired chants of an utter resignation and grandeur which noticeably influenced the music of the neighbouring lands. The extraordinary melodic wealth of these Hussite hymns enriched the Lutheran chorales of Germany and, later, the chants of the Moravian Brotherhood, and can even be traced in the hymns of the Hernhutters of the eighteenth century.

One of the most famous Hussite hymns, "Kdož jsú Boží bojovníci", ("Ye who strive for God") has played an important role in the history of the Czech people and was taken as a theme by — among other composers — both Smetana and Dvořák, appearing in the symphonic poem "Tábor" by the former and in the "Husitská Overtura" of his younger contemporary.

The Hussite movement, however, exerted a too one-sided effect on the evolution of Czech music, while at the same time communication with foreign sources was almost completely interrupted. Not until the reigns of George of Podiebrad (1458—1471) and the first Habsburgs (1526—1600) was there a renewed opportunity for the exchange of ideas and developments with the musical world outside. Then the new link with the Netherlands brought the polyphonic notation to Bohemia, where groups of singers (a sort of choral society, generally organized by a religious body) maintained the tradition of church music now adapted to the new poly-

2

THE HUSSITE HYMN "KDOŽ JSÚ BOŽÍ BOJOVNÍCI"

phony. The works of the great fifteenth and sixteenth century composers such as Jacobus Obrecht, Josquin des Prés and Orlando di Lasso, with their complicated polyphonic notation, put the technical proficience of the Czech singers to a stern test. None but the most perfectly trained professional choirs engaged in these performances, and so arose a great number of private choirs attached to the households of wealthy nobles which, side by side with the choirs of churches and monasteries, nurtured the musical life of the country. The court choirs of the Emperors Ferdinand I

3

and Maximilian II were famed at home and abroad. This flourishing period reached its climax in Prague during the reign of the extraordinary Habsburg monarch, Rudolph II (1575—1612). Rudolph was a fantastic personality, strongly attracted by the occult, and showing great appreciation and a profound knowledge of music, in addition to magic and astrology. He selected his court musicians with the same fastidious care and taste that he devoted to choosing an art treasure. A story is told that when one evening shortly before his death, his choir gave an exceptionally fine performance of a "Miserere" beneath his windows in the Hradčany Palace, he ordered that the singers be given their pay in full forthwith and also, notwithstanding the permanently impoverished state of his treasury, receive a handsome gift as well.

In 1568 Philippus de Monte, one of the most important "Dutchmen", was made head of the Imperial Court Choir. From many lands musicians flocked to Prague. The brothers Hans Leo and Jakob Hasler from Nuremberg; the Frenchmen Jacques Regard and Jean de Castro; the Southern Netherlanders, Carolus Luyton, Lambertus de Savije and Willem Formelis; the Italians Francesco Turini, Zanetti and Orologio, to name but a few found engagements of long or short duration in the Prague musical world, and even settled there. Prague had other attractions for musicians than the appointments to the Imperial Court. Jacobus Gallus (d. 1591), who came from Carinthia and was also known as Handl, became Cantor of the Church of Saint John. Several of the works of this great master of polyphony were printed with imperial consent.

This glorious period came to an abrupt and untimely end when the Emperor Matthias, successor to Rudolph, transferred his capital to Vienna and the concurrently altered political situation brought about a decline in every aspect of Czech life. At about this time the composer Jan Trojan Turnovský was writing chorales for male voices in five or six parts, which may be considered as musical curiosities of the time. Two other representatives of Czech composition of the latter half of the seventeenth century were Jiří Rychnovský (d. 1676), and his son Václav, who was well known as an organist in Prague.

We now come to the period of the figured bass and find the names of a few masters which will not mean much to us but which, in the lifetime of their bearers, were well known in all the musical centres of Europe. There was, for example, Jan Dismas Zelenka (1679—1745), a pupil of Antonio Lotti and J. J. Fux of Vienna, who later, in Dresden, composed church music which was highly thought of by Bach.

During this politically troubled period in Bohemia, music was one of

4

the few branches of the cultural life which continued to bear fruit. Apart from the activities of Czech composers at home, there was an extensive body of work produced by exiles and emigrants, which will be mentioned later, on account of its importance in the history of musical development. Even abroad, Zelenka retained his feeling of Czech nationality and among his compositions is a motet on a text in his native tongue and a suite for orchestra in which Czech themes are adapted. One of the forerunners of the Czech pre-classical style was the founder of the Prague School of Organists, Bohuslav Černohorský (1684—1742), who spent his youth in Italy as a member of the Minorite Order and taught Tarkini at Padua. The "Bohemian Bach", as he was called by his countrymen, had an exceptional gift for the composition of fugues, contriving to unite the melodiousness of the Italian with the contrapuntal proficiency of the central German organ music into a wholly individual style. Themes taken from Czech folksongs also form an element in his harmonious and delightful compositions, of which, unfortunately, but few survive. Černohorsky played a very important role as the teacher of a whole generation of musicians, amongst whom were Jan Zach (d. 1773), a notable composer for organ, and Gluck, who studied under him during his sojourn in Prague.

Alongside this activity in the field of instrumental music, the influence of oratorio and opera, coming mostly via Italy, began to make itself felt to a considerable degree. Dating from the beginning of the eighteenth century, Italian oratorios by Italian composers and sacred musical plays, in fact operas, were given regular performances under the auspices of the Jesuits and Piarists. Apart from Zelenka, it was as a rule German Bohemians who followed, or endeavoured to follow, in the footsteps of their foreign predecessors. Anton Tauber, choirmaster of the Saint Loretto Choir of Prague, composed German oratorios, one of the more striking titles of which deserves mention as a curiosity. What can be made of this subject, taken from the composer's text: "Der im bittern cypristrautenreichen Weingebirge Engaddi verlassene Brautigam"? ("The bridegroom abandoned among the wine mountains of Engardy, so beloved for their abundance of bitter cypresses").

As well as a "Bohemian Bach" there was a "Bohemian Handel", Johann Habermann (1706—1783), from whose Masses the real Handel did not find it beneath his dignity to copy passages for himself at one time or another. As in most of the central European countries at that period, there was in Bohemia a host of composers whose church music bears the impress of the Italian Baroque style. Though there were undoubtedly men of talent among them, yet, for the greater part, there is a lack of individuality.

A handful of Czech emigrants, however, had a great influence on the development of pre-classical music in Europe. The Benda family is an outstanding example. František Benda (1709—1786), from Benátky in Bohemia, is one of the most important representatives of the so-called "Berlin School". He died in Potsdam, where he was musical director at the Court of Frederick the Great, and was an associate of musicians such as Carl Philipp Emanuel Bach, Joachim Quanta and Johann Gottlieb Braun, whose circle shed brilliance on the musical court of the composer and flautist king. His younger brother, Jiří, or Georg, Benda (1722—1795), who was his superior in creative talent, was choirmaster at the court of Gotha from 1750 onwards. Among his compositions are the melodramas "Ariadne of Naxos" and "Media", composed in 1774 and 1775, which stand out for their use of the dramatic recitative and the then exceptionally vivid and picturesque orchestral accompaniment, which even evoked the admiration of Mozart. His compositions for voice contain arias of a dramatic intensity which seem, as in "Der Dorfjahrmarkt" of 1775, to anticipate Beethoven's "Fidelio". Benda was spiritually akin to Voltaire and Rousseau and exhibited many of the independent and peculiar traits of Beethoven, witness his Piano Concerto in G of 1788, one of his most mature compositions.

Another colony of Czech musicians was to be found in Mannheim, where Jan Václav Stamic, or Johann Wenzel Stamitz (1717—1757), had settled. There was a vigorous cultural life in this town, the most important of the Palatinate, and, in addition to Stamitz, several of his compatriots contributed to the musical activities there, among them František Xaverius Richter (1709—1789) and Antonín Filtz (1730—1760). These musicians, known as the "Mannheimers", acquired the reputation of being innovators in orchestration. They worked for unanimity and exactitude of interpretation and especially for the practice of dynamic change, developing the crescendo and decrescendo in place of the earlier register-dynamics which had precluded any gradation, 'forte' following directly upon 'piano' and *vice versa*, without transition. While these developments were not complete novelties, they in any case, achieved here a hitherto unknown mastery.

Stamitz was also one of the first important composers in the pre-classical style. It was perhaps František Miča (1694—1744), a musician in the service of the wealthy, dilettante nobleman Jan Adam von Questenberk, of Jaroměřice, whose influence is apparent in the work of Stamitz and Richter, both of whom spent a part of their youth in the neighbourhood where he was living. It is certainly worthy of note that while the style of

Miča's operas, oratorios and cantatas is close to that of Antonio Caldara, his first sinfonias indicate already a strong inclination towards the pre-classical.

While the Bendas and Stamitz pursued their musical careers abroad, the works of Brizi and his school introduced the pre-classical style in Bohemia and Moravia. In this way the music lovers of Prague received a considerable preparation for the art of Mozart, and the enthusiastic reception accorded to the presentation of "Le Nozze di Figaro" and "Don Giovanni" (the latter having been composed expressly for performance in Prague) at the Nostic Theatre is the more readily to be understood. Beethoven also met with early appreciation in the Czech capital.

Josef Mysliveček (1737—1781) was a much loved figure in Italy, where he lived from 1763 until his death in Rome. The popularity of his operas (numbering approximately thirty in all) was so great that he acquired the appellation "Il divino Boemo" and himself adopted the Italian version of his name, "Venatorini", in place of Mysliveček, which means "little huntsman". Italian melodiousness was allied with Czech temperament to produce in his work a style that, above all in the sinfonias, sonatas and string quartets, resembles that of the early Mozart. The young genius from Salzburg was a friend of Mysliveček and esteemed his work to the extent of being influenced by it, particularly in his early compositions.

In Vienna also there were a number of composers of Czech origin, some of whom enjoyed during their lifetime a considerable reputation. The names of Jan Vaňhal, or Wanhal (1739—1813), Leopold Kozeluch (1752—1818) and Vojtěch Jírovec, or Adalbert Gyrowetz (1763—1850), were mentioned in the same breath as those of the great masters. Now their slight, at best agreeably melodious works are completely forgotten. Václav Jan Tomášek (1774—1850), a splendid pianist and teacher but a mediocre composer, and Dionys Weber were two fanatical admirers of Mozart who had scarcely any appreciation at all for Beethoven after his very early period. A much more interesting and original figure was the widely travelled piano virtuoso Jan Ladislav Dusík, or Dussek (1761—1812). His work was very uneven, but the capricious and romantic temper, the often daring modulations and the advanced chromatics that characterize his best compositions, render them vital and attractive to this day. Antonín Rejcha (1770—1836), who, like Dussek, lived in Paris, was a teacher of composition at the Conservatoire. His most notable accomplishments were in the field of theory and one of his many works, his "Traité de Haute Composition Musicale", ("Treatise on Classical Musical Composition") which was translated into German by Czerny, was adopted as the standard text-book on the subject in most of the music schools of Europe. Among the many brilliant pupils of this eminent pedagogue was César Franck, who, as a boy of fourteen, came to Rejcha for instruction during the last year of the latter's life.

The resurgance of Czech nationalism coincided with the first years of the romantic movement in Europe. An event of far-reaching consequence was the discovery of the "Königinhofer Handschrift" — later found to have been forged by Václav Hanka and his friends. The effects of this document, with its contents of literary and historical interest, apparently dating from the Middle Ages, was to rouse in the Czech people a passionate interest in the past of their nation. A Czech equivalent of "Des Knaben Wunderhorn" ("The Magic Flute") by the two German romantics Achim von Arnim and Clemens Brentano was the collection of ballads "Kytica" ("Bouquet") published in 1853 by Karel J. Erben (1811—1870); while the series of Czech folk songs and fairy stories of the same publisher was invaluable as a literary stimulus for composers.

The first representative of the Czech national revival in the field of music was the composer František Škroup (1801—1862), famous for his "Kde domov můj" ("Where is my Native land?"), which has become a national song. The operetta from which it comes, "Fidlovačka" ("The Fair") had, despite its sweetly sentimental, only faintly Slavonic music and harmless libretto, an electric effect on the political feelings of its audience. At the time of his death in Rotterdam, Škroup was chorusmaster of the German Opera. In 1935 the Czech government commemorated the centenary of the composition of his great success with a ceremony at his grave in the city where he died in the midst of his work.

In 1826 Škroup composed the first Czech opera, "Dráteník" ("The Faggot Binder"), which met with resounding success. He also turned to history for subjects for his two tragic operettas, "Oldřich and Božena" and "The Marriage of Libuše". But it remained for Smetana to be the first composer whose talent and power to render the epic justified him in the choice of such themes from Czech history as form the subjects of his operas "Dalibor" and "Libuše".

In all events the time had come after an era of making shift with translated operas, which often suffered strange transformations, for instance, Weigl's popular "Schweizerfamilie" (which became a family of Slovaks from the Tatras mountains) — when original texts in the Czech tongue were ready to hand. With this material, through the medium of Smetana's genius, the Czech national opera was to be raised from a state of good-natured dilettantism to artistic and cultural value.

# BEDŘICH SMETANA

AT the time of Smetana's birth, in 1824, the work of most European composers was of a pronouncedly romantic character. Franz Schubert, one of the most famous of the early Romantics, was making feverish use of the last four years of his short life to produce his greatest works, while his older contemporary, Beethoven, was withdrawing into the abstract world of his chamber music, of which the testament, his last five string quartets, realizes the essence of loneliness in terms of music. The master of romantic opera, Carl Maria von Weber, in this the last year of his life, was inspired by Shakespeare's fairyland to compose his "Oberon". The great figures of the following generation, Robert Schumann, Felix Mendelssohn, Frédéric Chopin, and Richard Wagner were coming to a realization of their powers. The polished Luigi Cherubini was at work on his most famous pieces in France where the strangest figure of the Romantic movement, Hector Berlioz, was shortly to reveal his bizarre genius. In the remotest corner of Smetana's native land, the child prodigy, Franz Liszt, was scoring his first successes as virtuoso pianist; and concert-goers everywhere in Europe were going into transports over Nicolo Paganini, the wizard of the violin.

The names of other internationally celebrated composers of this period must not be forgotten. There were Rossini, Bellini, Donizetti, Spontini, Meyerbeer, Halévy, Auber and more, whose exceedingly popular works kept the opera houses of Europe filled to overflowing. Besides the great Pole Chopin, who has already been mentioned, the outstanding talents from the Slavonic countries, exclusive of Bohemia, were his compatriot Stefan Moniuszko, who composed the opera "Halka", and the Russians, Michael Glinka and Alexander Dargomysjki, whose compositions were likewise largely operatic.

Smetana's lifetime, thus, coincided with the flowering of the mid-nineteenth century Romantic movement, a period of great artistic activity

9

which has left to posterity many works of lasting cultural value. Here is a far from complete list of his contemporaries: the musicians Richard Wagner, Anton Bruckner, Johannes Brahms, Peter Cornelius, Franz Liszt, Johann and Jozef Strauss, César Franck, Eduard Lalo, Giuseppe Verdi and Jacques Offenbach; the literary figures Friedrich Hebbel, Gottfried Keller, Conrad Ferdinand Meyer, Gustave Flaubert, Edmond and Jules de Goncourt, Leconte de Lisle, Charles Dickens, Robert and Elizabeth Browning, Alfred Tennyson, Dante Gabriel Rossetti, George Meredith, Walt Whitman, Hendrik Ibsen, Björnstjerne Björnson, Fedor Dostojevski, Leo Tolstoy, Jan Neruda — one of the great Czech poets and novelists who has frequently been compared to Gottfried Keller — and Vítězslav Hálek, a popular lyrical poet in whose verses Smetana and Dvořák and countless other composers found such happy inspiration. The greatest Czech painter of the 19th century, Josef Manes, was also at this time at the height of his powers.

Bedřich (Frederick) Smetana was born on March 2nd, 1824 at Litomyšl, a small town in eastern Bohemia, almost on the Moravian border. His father, František, chief fireman in the service of Graf Waldstein, had a fairly eventful life behind him and had known many changes of fortune when, in 1820, he took as his third wife Barbara Link, the daughter of a coachman in the employ of a nobleman of Hořice. The future composer was the first son of his three marriages to be born to the elder Smetana, and the story goes that when the servant brought him the glad tidings he sprang up and performed a dance of joy in the courtyard of the inn — which dance was, as a matter of course, a polka, the favourite of all good Bohemians.

Young Bedřich grew up in a happy, unusually musical home. He was taught to play both piano and violin and as a child wonder of six performed before a group of local gentry, executing with radiant self-confidence an arrangement for clavicord of the Overture to Bellini's "I Puritani". When he was a little older, his family moved to Jindřichův-Hradec, a town on the highway between Prague and Vienna. This particular stretch of country, rich in historical landmarks and charming scenery, must certainly have furnished Smetana with the material, reworked in the light of fond memory, for the cycle of tone poems "Má Vlast" which he composed in the last years of his life.

After attending several schools, where he evidently devoted much more energy to musical subjects than to the acquisition of general knowledge he was sent to Pilsen to study under the vigilant eye of an uncle. Even here, however, musical pursuits soon gained the upper hand. He was

SMETANA'S BIRTHPLACE IN LITOMYŠL

next enrolled at the Academic Gymnasium at Prague, which represented the penultimate step in the usual humanistic education. Here the director, the famous 19th century Slavophile Josef Jungmann, inculcated in his pupil an undying enthusiasm for the cause of the Czech national revival. But when the father appeared in person to make enquiries about the progress of his son, the worthy doctor had to confess that the boy had not been seen in the classroom for months. Bedřich was sent back to Pilsen where, to the general astonishment, he passed his final examinations.

Overcoming the manifold objections on the part of his father, the successful scholar then departed for Prague to take up the study of music in earnest. Full of confidence, he wrote in his journal: "With the blessing of God, I may become a Liszt in technique, a Mozart in composition." He had money enough for the journey, beyond that he would have to support himself.

The attraction of Prague for Smetana lay not only in that it was the musical centre of Bohemia but in the presence there of Katharina Kolář, a young lady from Pilsen with whom he had become acquainted when at school there. In Prague his love for her decided him in studying with the blind Josef Proksch, a well known instructor of the day, of whom Katharina had for some time been a pupil, rather than at the Conservatorium which was, in any case, considered reactionary by the younger musicians.

Smetana and Katharina were married after a lengthy engagement, but this eventual realization of their dreams was only made possible by the good offices of Franz Liszt, a man whose ready helpfulness and idealistic

11

nature won him the gratitude of so many musicians of his time. The two young people had been living in precarious enough circumstances in the years before their marriage, but in 1848, with the moral and material support of Liszt, Smetana was able to open a music school.

However, the time before had not been lost; his experiences had borne fruit in creation. In 1844, inspired by his love for Katharina, he wrote "Bagatelles et Impromptus", which in form and type of subject reflect the influence of Schumann's programme pieces. His "Six Morceaux Charactéristiques" Op. 1, addressed to Liszt with an appeal for help, were considered by the latter as the most strikingly individual composition to come to his attention for a long time. In the same spirit were the six "Stambuchblätter", Op 2; again the influence of Schumann's rich harmonic structure here endows the comparatively unstudied melody with depth and substance, particularly in Op. 1. But the qualities which set it apart from the rather lightweight salon pieces of the time, and which Liszt found so individual, now appear little more than derivative.

These promising beginnings can be viewed in the light of the four comparatively tranquil years in which they were made, during which Smetana was a music teacher in the household of Graf Thun. In less peaceful circumstances appeared the compositions, "The Marches" of the rebellious student corps, and "Nationale Guarde", written in 1848, the year that saw the revolt in every land of those groups now known as oppressed minorities. A "Festival Overture", his first work for orchestra, dates from the same year, and in 1853 he wrote a "Triumph Symphony" in celebration of the wedding of the Emperor Franz Jozef to Princess Elizabeth of Bavaria. In 1882 he revised this four-part work, of which the scherzo still stands in its own right as a fine piece, but the symphony never became popular as programme music.

His first really considerable work, composed only two years later, was the Trio for violin, cello and piano, in G Minor Op. 15, written in memory of his oldest daughter Friederike, a musically gifted child whom he lost in 1855. This piece is a typical example of the Romantic music of the middle of the last century. This period is caracterized (also as far as other art forms are concerned) by a strong inclination to pathos, as well in the heroic as in the lyric genre.

The ever present danger of turgidity and sentimentality, not completely avoided by even the greatest composers, was a pitfall for their colleagues of lesser stature.

For some time it has been a convention — fortunately now being abandoned — to treat composers of the second rank with a sort of good-

12

natured condescension. It must not, after all, be forgotten that a composer who essayed to reach the highest but whose achievement fell short of that of Bach, Mozart, Brückner or Wagner may yet be accounted of great stature in the musical world. Even those who find their place in the third rank are not by any means all Tosellis and Ketelbeys. Smetana and Dvořák, however dissimilar in endowment and development, belong among the minor masters when measured against the sublime figures named above. Nevertheless they were both great composers. In his "Prodaná Nevěsta", ("The Bartered Bride") Smetana wrote an opera of a brilliance, clarity, and warmth that compares with Mozart's "Le Nozze di Figaro" and has hardly been equalled since. And there occur in the chamber music of Dvořák certain slow passages which for intensity of feeling must be placed among the greatest music of the kind. Edvard Grieg falls into the same class, to make comparisons with an artist of about the same importance — a man whom we feel to be a great composer because he has been able to create something like the slow middle passages of his Piano Concerto. The less successful works of Smetana and Dvořák fall far short — particularly in the case of Dvořák — of the level of their great compositions: in other words the quality of their work taken as a whole does not entitle them to a place among the greatest artists of their time.

To return to the Trio in G, this composition is one of the most charming of Smetana's early period. The ambitious opening, moderato assai, in G minor, 3/4 time, is permeated with an elegaic mournfulness which gently moderates in the course of the movement. An allegro ma non agitato, in G minor, 2/4 time, follows and a Scherzo which, in the pattern set by Schumann, contains two trios, here called Alternativo I and Alternativo II. The last movement is a Presto in G minor, changing to G major, in 6/8 and 2/4 time. This work, the theme of which in the programmatic sense is the slow overcoming of a deep grief, is saved from its overflowing romanticism by the unmistakable power and passionate sincerity of the poetic feeling with which it is charged. The influence of Schumann is still strong but there are certain arabesques and harmonic combinations that make it easy to believe that Smetana, who was also a pianist in the virtuoso class, enjoyed the reputation of being a most sensitive interpreter of Chopin.

In the reactionary period which followed the revolutionary year of 1848 Smetana, with his partisanship for the cause of Czech nationalism, found it hard to breathe freely in his native land. In spirit his music allied itself increasingly to the guiding principles of Liszt and his followers. Having encountered nothing more than polite reserve at the home of Schumann and his wife, he found on the other hand, at the famous Hungarian's at Weimar a common sympathy in aims and ideas. He became, and remained to the end of his life, a convinced follower of the so-called "New German School", against which Johannes Brahms and his circle arrayed themselves in the publication of their rather unfortunately worded manifesto of 1860.

In 1856 the Harmoniska Sällskapet of Göteborg in Sweden offered Smetana the post of director. He accepted with alacrity and departed for the Scandinavian trading city with a sense of relief, arriving in October, 1856. As conductor, he was able to present at choice, choral works of the classic and romantic schools and succeeded beyond his most extravagant hopes in bringing what he called the "antediluvian taste" of the citizens of Göteborg up to date. The more practical results of his position and his everyday contact with the orchestra were the three symphonic poems he composed in Sweden. "Richard III" dating from 1858, "Valdštýnův Tábor" ("Wallenstein's Camp"), from the following year, and "Haakon Jar", composed in 1861. Here the influence of Liszt is unmistakable, extending even to the choice of subject; Smetana also turned to literature for his themes, to Shakespeare for the sinister figure of Richard III, to Schiller, adapting the third part of his "Wallenstein's Lager" and to the works of the then famous Danish tragic poet, Adam Gottlob Öhlenschläger (1779—1850). Though the pattern set by Liszt is faithfully followed in the design, and limits the inventiveness of these compositions, the development of the themes and the expressiveness of the music have a definite interest of their own.

The military defeat inflicted on Austria by Italy in 1859, forced the central government in Vienna to take a more liberal attitude towards the political aspirations of the several non-Germanic peoples belonging to the empire. As a result, a general revival took place in Prague, which saw the founding of a Czech union of singers under the name Hlahol ("Sound"), and the Umělecká Beseda ("Artists' League"), the music branch of which was exceedingly active. The revival of enthusiasm and interest gave the spur to further initiative; with what means could be collected, a temporary theatre was constructed, in which, on November 18th, 1862, the opening performance was given. The existence of an orchestra attached to the Czechoslovakian opera also made symphony concerts a possibility, and a nationally inspired musical life, hitherto rendered impossible by circumstances, began to flourish in all directions.

Smetana now realized that he had a place to fill in Prague. In May, 1861, he gave up his good position at Göteborg and returned to the land of his birth, where he was made heartily welcome by the leaders of the

THE 'TEMPORARY' THEATRE IN PRAGUE (1863—1881)

new Czech literary movement, Hálek and Neruda. He entered upon a period of incredible activity, becoming conductor of the Symphony Orchestra, director of the Hlahol and, in 1866, conductor at the Opera. He was on the board of the Umělecká Beseda and wrote reviews for Národní Listy, the organ of the Czech National Party. At the same time the nationalistic orientation of his own composition at last began to manifest itself fully.

Before passing on to the subject of his work, the personal life of Smetana must be given a little attention. His wife Katharina, whose frail health had proved unequal to the northern climate of Göteborg, had died at Dresden in April, 1859, when the family was on the way to take the annual holiday in Bohemia. She had borne her husband four daughters of whom all but one died in childhood. Smetana did not remain a widower for long, marrying for the second time in July, 1860, Betti Fernandi, the sister of his brother Karel's wife, whom he had met while on a visit to his brother. She presented him with two more daughters who grew up happily with the one surviving from the first marriage. Betti Smetana outlived her husband by twenty four years, dying in 1908 at the age of sixty-eight.

Prior to his departure for Göteborg, Smetana had already written some dances of a definitely Slavonic character such as "Trois Polkas de Salon",

15

Op. 7 and "Trois Polkas Poétiques", Op. 8 (1855). "Souvenir de Bohème en Forme de Polka", in two parts, Op. 12 and Op. 13, followed in 1863. The extent to which Smetana's work takes its inspiration from folk music is illustrated by his use of the Polka. The Polka (actually půlka or half-step) was a round dance in fast 2/4 time which had become fashionable everywhere in Bohemia in the first half of the 18th century, swiftly taking its place as the leading national dance. Both Smetana, in his "České tance" and Dvořák in his two part "Slovanské Tance, Op. 46 add 72" used the majority of the Czechoslovak national folk dance forms — as did Chopin with the Mazurka, the Polonaise and the Waltz — endowing them with a formalization and style in the process of rendering them in terms of instrumental music.

A survey of the most important dance forms will be opportune here. After the Polka, the Furiant was certainly the most popular. Furiant suggests a braggard, a vainglorious fellow, and there is indeed a challenging spirit to this quickstep with its sharp accents and changing ryhthms. (Türk in his "Klavierschule", of 1789, calls this dance "Furie", so it is possible that the name is of Latin origin.) The Sousedská (from "soused" meaning "neighbour") corresponds closely to the South German and Austrian Ländler which was originally, as the name shows, a country dance. The Ländler appears in a refined form in the works of Schubert and is also clearly the origin of the trio of the minuet which occurs in the symphonies of Haydn. Later composers like Bruckner and Mahler adapted the Ländler, each in his own manner, as trios in the scherzos of their symphonies. There were, further, the Skočná, a jumping dance in quick 2/4 time; the Kolovrat, a spinning-wheel dance in 3/8 time; and several others whose names more or less make their nature clear, such as the Medvěd, or bear dance, Oves, meaning oats, which was connected with the harvest festival, the onion dance, the chicken dance and so forth.

Soon after his return to Prague, Smetana began to look about for a suitable text for an opera, finally receiving the historical libretto "Braniboři v Čechách" ("The Brandenburgs in Bohemia") from Karel Sabina. The story is set in the early 14th century, and Smetana found in it, despite the rather indifferent text, a gratifying opportunity to depict the Prussian invaders and his own gallant countrymen, with the traditional pair of young lovers in their midst. Considering his close contact with Liszt and his circle of Wagner lovers, it is hardly surprising that the composer took, as model for this work, the operas of Wagner's middle period. However the extensive part of the score devoted to choruses takes a highly individual, moderately nationalistic form. Though this work was completed in

16

1862 the première took place only in January 1866, under the direction of the composer himself. In May of the same year, the work which has given Smetana his greatest claim to fame, the comic opera "Prodaná Nevěsta" ("The Bartered Bride") was performed for the first time.

Not since Mozart's "Le Nozze di Figaro" had there been anything in opera to compare with this, so sparkling and graceful, of such admirable vitality, both delicate and robust. Smetana's sensitive, almost childishly gay and optimistic nature, which had buoyed him up under many blows of fate, here enabled him to create a triumphantly lovely work of art. From the brilliant overture to the last curtain, an uninterrupted stream of superb music holds the hearer entranced.

The story of this delightful masterpiece concerns the troubles that beset two young lovers, Jeník and Mařenka. The marriage broker, Kecal, with his oily tongue and peasant cunning, persuades Mařenka's parents to betroth her to the shy stuttering Vašek, the son of the peasant Tobias Mícha by his second marriage. On her birthday Kecal reveals to Mařenka a document in which her father has signed his agreement to her marriage with the son of Tobias Mícha, but Mařenka still hopes to dissuade Vašek by telling him that there is another girl who truly loves him. Meanwhile, Kecal has approached Jeník with the offer of another bride (whose virtues he is never tired of proclaiming) and the sum of a hundred guilders if he will renounce Mařenka. Jeník answers that the sum is far too small but, when he hears that Mařenka is promised away from him, agrees to withdraw for three hundred guilders and a written agreement that no one but the son of Tobias Mícha shall get her. News of this gets about and the whole village is enraged that Jeník has bartered his bride for the sum of three hundred guilders. Poor silly Vašek meanwhile lives in a state of terror that Mařenka will poison him, as she has threatened to do. Of course Mařenka hears of Jeník's faithlessness and refuses to listen to his explanation; in despair she is ready to marry Vašek after all, and, when Jeník insists that Tobias Míchas' son loves her more than anyone else in the world, she is overborne. Meanwhile, Jeník calls upon Kecal to fulfill the terms of his contract with him. The denouément, of course, is that Jeník turns out to be the son of Tobias Mícha by his first marriage, and the opera comes to a happy end for all except the discomfited Kecal.

The author of the libretto, again Karel Sabina, is to be thanked for creating the priceless Kecal, a figure which makes him worthy to be called a Czech Dickens. But what an infinite debt is owed to Smetana for his splendid music, for the individual use of folk song and dance, for the genuine feeling which colours the light-hearted as well as the more serious

KECAL'S ARIA (GERMAN TRANSLATION), ACT I OF "THE BARTERED BRIDE"

MANUSCRIPT OF A PAGE FROM "THE BARTERED BRIDE"

moments, and above all, for the inexhaustible freshness and resourcefulness which make "Prodaná Nevěsta" a masterpiece of the first order. The vivacious, whirling spirit of the overture may well stand comparison with that of "Le Nozze di Figaro". Smetana's great gift for constructing a striking architectonic effect is demonstrated throughout. Every finale is the culmination of an unbroken flow of dramatically developing music. At the end of the first act, all the musical elements of the preceding scenes are gathered into the joyous strains of the famous Polka in C, which, with the Furiant of the first part of the second act, is one of the two most exhilara-

19

TRIO FROM THE FURIANT IN "THE BARTERED BRIDE"

ting dances in opera. The Meno Vivo, the section comparable to the trio in a scherzo clearly illustrates, in turn, the unusual talent for subtle harmony which was an integral part of Smetana's music. The daring and original treatment, as for example in the boldly dissonant anticipations, is reminiscent of some of the Ländler trios in Mahler's symphonies, of which, in fact, these passages of Smetana's seem almost to be the prototype. Such a supposition rests on fairly secure ground, since Mahler, with his acquisitive temperament, gathered up and re-worked in his own way innumerable diverse musical influences. Also it is known that he was particularly fond of the folk music of the Slavonic lands under Austrian

20

domination, probably owing to the fact that his boyhood was passed in Moravia. His admiration for Smetana's work was also indicated by the fact that shortly after being appointed director of the Viennese Opera he introduced "Dalibor" as the first novelty on his programme.

Among the strikingly original passages of the opera is the trio of Kecal, Ludmila and Krušina ("Gekommen wär er mit mir wie gerne") ("How did he enjoy coming with me?") in the first act; finally, the sheer beauty of choruses and arias, exemplified by the sextet from the third act and Mařenka's wonderfully moving aria towards the end of the opera, place it among the leading works of the last century for its lyrical qualities alone.

The next to follow in the train of succesful operas initiated by "The Brandenburgs in Bohemia" was "Dalibor", on which Smetana began to work in 1866, directly after the lively music of the opera buffa, "The Bartered Bride". This is a tragedy, its story based on the old Czech tale of Dalibor, a national hero. The original German text by Wenzig was translated into Czech for the libretto. As the legend goes, Dalibor was imprisoned for avenging the murder of his greatest friend, whose sister, Milada, falls in love with him and tries to save him from the consequences of his deed. She gains entrance to his dungeon in the Hradčany, bringing with her a magic violin with which the prisoner can communicate with the spirit of his dead friend. When, in their attempt to escape, Milada appears to be fatally wounded, Dalibor kills himself in despair. This opera expounds the theme of national freedom and may be seen as a revolutionary piece comparable to "La Muette de Portici". In its aesthetic and deeply human values it can also be likened to "Fidelio", while, musically, it exhibits a wholeness of style and mood which recall "Lohengrin". The principal motif, in G, is the mainspring of all the others and characterizes not so much the person of the hero as the entire underlying theme of the opera.

This work brought into the open the struggle between the progressives and the reactionaries in the Prague musical world. The spokesman of the latter group, the singing-master František Pivoda, was one of Smetana's bitterest enemies, though at the time of the première of "The Brandenburgs in Bohemia" he had written: "The work of Smetana is destined to be the cornerstone of the edifice of Czech national opera." The two most important of Smetana's admirers were Ludwig Procházka and a certain prominent musician, music historian and art-lover, Otakar Hostinský, both of whom took up arms for Wagner and Smetana. An important music periodical of the time went so far as to adopt the name "Dalibor" as a sign of its sympathies, and Smetana himself always considered this one of his important works.

FINALE OF "THE BARTERED BRIDE"

In 1871, to the immense gratification of the nationalistic feeling of the Czech people, the Emperor Franz Jozef proposed to have himself crowned king of Bohemia. The universal rejoicing connected with the approach of this event, in which Smetana participated to the full extent of his ardent nature, was the occasion for him to undertake a long-cherished project, an opera based on a text, again by Wenzig, of which the subject was the legendary national heroine Libuše. According to the legend, this princess built the city of Prague and, through her union with the peasant leader Přemysl, founded the first line of Czech rulers. Smetana termed his work "Slavná", that is to say a festival tableau; his precise intention can best be described by quoting what he himself wrote about Libuše: "Libuše is not written for regular performance during the opera season; it is rather my wish that it be reserved for suitable occasions of national celebration."

Compared with "Dalibor", "Libuše" shows a great advance in symphonic structure, particularly in the polyphonous forms of the score and the remarkably fine harmonization and instrumentation. The characteristics of Czech folk songs have an important effect here in that the recitative is made to conform to the peculiarities of the language. Smetana had read and taken to heart Hostinský's essay on the necessity in a national music for accord between the rhythm of the music and the accentuation of the language.

Meanwhile the anticipated coronation of the Emperor failed to take place and Smetana completed his work without any definite occasion for its performance in sight; the première took place only in 1881.

After these two great historical tragic operas, Smetana again turned his eyes towards a different, less serious subject, partly for relief from the emotional stress he had felt while composing the tragedies, partly because of the greater chance of early production afforded to work in a lighter vein. He found, in a version by Zungel of a one-act French comedy, the story for "Dvě Vdovy" ("The Two Widows"), a light opera in the style of those being produced with success by Auber at that time in France. It concerns a young widow whose steadfast resolve to remain faithful to the memory of her husband blights the love of a new suitor in the bud. However, the machinations of her friends and well-wishers conquer her scruples and it all comes to a happy end. Smetana knew well how to render the atmosphere of the little castle which is the setting of the piece with a sure and playful touch. A more romantic and less profound feeling, as compared with the musical qualities of "The Bartered Bride", is the most notable feature of this operetta.

In the years between 1868 and 1874 Smetana was at the height of his creative powers and, by virtue of his inborn optimism and enterprise, might have rested secure for many years to come from the uncertainties of the artist's life, had not deafness, the greatest calamity that can befall a musician, slowly begun to undermine his very existence. Early in 1874 the following notice appeared in the periodical "Dalibor": "Owing to a condition of nervous strain brought on by the unceasing annoyance proceeding recently from a certain quarter, the Director of the Orchestra, Bedřich Smetana, is forced to withdraw completely for an indefinite period from all musical and cultural activities".

Apart from the relentless attacks of his enemies, there was another factor which undoubtedly contributed to his distressed condition, namely the overwhelming accumulation of positions and responsibilities which had become a burden too great for one man to bear.

His deafness — according to medical opinion, of nervous origin, not actually an organic defect — made its appearance in the summer of 1874, when he discovered that a note of music registered differently in each ear and began to experience a persistent ringing in the ears and the reverberation through his head of the treble chord of the A major sixth, an indescribable torment for a composer. Finally, in the night of the 19th of October, 1874, he became completely deaf. This great misfortune naturally brought in its train every kind of practical difficulty. He wrote to an old

BEDŘICH SMETANA (1874)

friend at Göteborg: "I am now utterly useless as far as practising my profession is concerned. My sources of livelihood have dried up and I am dependent on the tiny pension voted to me by the directors of the opera in recognition of my services to the national music". This pension amounted to 1,200 guilders a year; fortunately his Swedish friends were able to collect a fairly respectable sum which helped him through the first difficult period.

Nevertheless it is truly a miracle that Smetana's unquenchable love of life and unbounded energy enabled him to rise above the disaster and engage anew in composition. Freed from the multitudinous and taxing duties connected with his position at the opera, he turned his attention to instrumental composition, which he had not undertaken since the three tone poems composed in Sweden. Between 1874 and 1875 he completed the first four parts of the symphonic cycle, "Má Vlast" ("My Fatherland"), designed as a hymn of praise to the cultural and legendary glories of his native land, and as an evocation of the beauty and poetry of the Czech countryside.

The first symphonic poem of the cycle is named "Vyšehrad" after an ancient Bohemian stronghold standing on a cliff above the Moldau to the south of Prague. Taking this mythical royal fortress of the Přemyslides as his symbol, Smetana evokes the glories of the past. The inspiration for this Vyšehrad motif came to him on the very day that he completely lost his hearing. Lumír, a legendary minstrel, plucking at the strings of his harp and telling of the past, is represented as the work opens with a passage of seemingly experimental chords in E; then horn and woodwind take up the motif followed by the strings. A new lyrical theme, in thirds, emerges after a passage of contrapuntal development, and borne by flutes, oboes and horns grows to a climax of full orchestra, and then dies softly away as the dream of past tumult and splendour fades.

24

"Vltava" ("The Moldau") is Smetana's best known and most popular work for orchestra and fully deserves the fame it enjoys. The fact that it makes little demand on the hearer in no way implies a lack of originality. Within the framework of a delicately romantic feeling for Nature, Smetana's great gift for imaginative and epic composition is amply demonstrated. The extensive notes which Smetana made to accompany the score, explain the significance of the successive musical episodes. They read: "The source of the Moldau; the first tributary, entrance of clarinets at the 16th bar; woods; hunt, following the reprise; country wedding, 2/4 time; Luna; dance of elves, fifth bar in A; the St. Johan Rapids, 33rd bar in 6/8 time; the wide curve of the Moldau, più mosso; Vyšehrad motif at the 69th bar, before finale".

Concerning the tone poem "Šárka" Smetana wrote: "In brief, this piece was inspired by the sight of the landscape at Šárka which brought to my mind the legendary maiden of the same name. It was not my intention to depict the wild and rocky valley near Prague but rather the legend connected with it". This is the rather long, involved tale of an Amazon-like figure, Šárka, by whose perfidy her upright and honourable lover Ctirad was destroyed.

This third poem of the cycle which, with its heavy emotional tone, comes perilously close to a full-blown Romanticism, is far inferior to the fourth "Z českých luhů a hájů" ("The Czech Fields and Forests"), one of the most beautiful of the odes to nature written by Smetana in tribute to his much-loved Bohemia.

These almost lyrical programme notes accompany the work: "After a moving opening in G, changing shortly from the minor to the major of the key, a fugue in 3/4 time, carried by the strings, introduces a mood of pastoral tranquility suggested by bird calls, repeated triplets and the clear, romantic notes of horn and clarinet to the effect that the atmosphere of the scene is completely realized. The air of a Polka then calls up the picture of a country fair, accompanied by all its familiar sounds, and the composition ends with a presto fortissimo passage on a note of jubilation". This fresh and captivating work can easily bear comparison with "The Moldau" and deserves to be heard as frequently as its popular sister piece.

While "The Moldau" and "The Czech Fields and Forests" extol the beauty of the Czech countryside, and "Vyšehrad" and "Šárka" are themes culled from the Czech sagas, the last two tone poems, "Tábor" and "Blaník", both commemorate landmarks in the actual course of Czech history. Tábor was the Hussite encampment on which spot a town of the same name later grew up; Blaník is a mountain in Bohemia in whose caverns, according to popular belief, the Hussite armies lie sleeping until the call to arms. These two parts of the cycle are closely linked, not only by their common musical atmosphere, but in sharing as principal motif the melody of the choral "Kdož jsú Boží bojovníci", In "Blaník" interest is provided by the contrast between the peaceful mountain landscape and the mysterious host deep in the mountainside; "Tábor", on the other hand, suffers from a lack of variety in melodic material, though the harmonic and rhythmic development of what there is is full of ingenuity. That "Šárka" and the two last-named parts of the cycle have never become regular items on concert programmes outside Czechoslovakia, can be explained by the fact that they make a somewhat exclusive appeal to those nationalistic feelings and interest of the hearers which were also one of the mainsprings of Smetana's work. The most inspired of the series are unquestionably "The Moldau", "The Czech Fields and Forests" and, to a barely lesser degree, "Vyšehrad". The "Vyšehrad" motif is in itself a gem which pleased Smetana so greatly that it makes its appearance at the climax of the "Moldau" and also, as a symbolic touch, in "Blaník".

Between 1876 and 1878, Smetana composed two more operas, "Hubička" ("The Kiss") and "Tajemství" ("The Secret"). "Hubička" is the first opera of his deafness, and is expressly entitled a folk operetta, which, in view of its utter stylistic simplicity, is quite fitting. Apart from a few passages of genuine lyrical beauty, it appears flat and conventional — though if heard in full performance, rather than in the form of the piano adaptation of the score (about the only way of becoming acquainted with any of Smetana's operas beyond "The Bartered Bride") it might prove charming enough. The libretto, an adaptation by Elise Krásnohorská of a novelette by Caroline Světlá, tells a simple village tale of a young widower whose new fianceé refuses to give him a kiss until they have been joined in church. Her superstition that such a premature kiss would offend the dead first wife provides the situation of the opera and, of course, is duly overcome by the time it reaches a happy end.

"The Secret" the libretto of which is also the work of Elise Krásnohorská, is a series of tableaux of life in a small Czech town; a comedy concerning two prominent figures of the town whose life-long feud is turned to friendship by the attachment of two of their children. The musical structure of this operetta is much more elaborate than that of its predecessor; the contrapuntal development of the melodies is full of spirit and fantasy and the careful handling of the choruses adds to the interest.

Also dating from the first years of Smetana's deafness is the String Quartet in E "Z mého Života" ("From my Life"), which he composed towards the

OPENING PASSAGE OF THE STRING QUARTET "FROM MY LIFE"

end of 1876. Smetana's somewhat naïve autobiographical notes, on which the work is based, were used with such artistry that an undoubted little master-piece of chamber music is the result. The ingenious references to his disturb-ed hearing by the high, shrill part written for the first violin — which describe the sensations he actually suffered — should not distract attention from the musically far more important mood of the composition, the roman-tic warmth and sincerity of which is intensified by the undertone of sorrow running throughout. Written long after the Trio in G, this quartet "From my Life" was still the first chamber music to express the Czech mood in a stylistically secure idiom, and it led the way to the creation of that body of chamber music to which, after Smetana, Dvořák above all would make such a royal contribution.

During this period Smetana also wrote some music for piano. The cycle "Rêves" belongs to the best and most individual of his piano works. The style of "Consolation" is fairly typical of his lyric works for piano; the influence of Chopin and Liszt is obvious, but the content is characteristic of Smetana. "In Bohemia" and "Country Festival in Bohemia" contain much material which had already appeared, in another form, in the country scenes of the operas and in "Má Vlast".

The Czech dances already mentioned were composed in 1879. Smetana took the many and very diverse national dances as subjects for a series of poetic and imaginative pieces. The first group consists of four polkas; the second is perhaps the most interesting of the series on account of its great originality and expressiveness. Altogether, they illustrate the extraordinary variety of rhythm and mood of the Czech folk dances. There is a certain distinctive delicacy and frequently, noble virtuosity about them that is sadly missed in Smetana's subsequent works of this kind.

We now come to the last years of the composer's life. His condition preyed upon him spiritually and physically. The mental concentration required for composition brought on, after barely an hour of work, such an unendurable state of congestion and ringing in the ears that he was often compelled to abandon the effort. His doctors, mindful of his deteriorating condition — he also suffered in an advanced degree from hardening of the arteries — had forbidden him any work which made great demands on his system. Nevertheless, his tremendous courage and optimism enabled him to triumph again, if only briefly, over his infirmities. In an astonishingly short time he completed his last opera "Čertova Stěna" ("The Devil's Wall"), based on a highly improbable and confused libretto by Elise Krásnohorská, which, considering the date of composition and the antecedents of Smetana, suggests in the harmonic treatment that he still had a fund of surprisingly modern ideas to draw upon.

A serious factor that now began to make itself felt was that he no longer had a true sense of the actual orchestral rendering of his music, which, though not limiting his inspiration, resulted in a definite sobering of his instrumental inventiveness, and inevitably robbed his work of much of its earlier brilliance. The première of "Čertova Stěna", which took place in the autumn of 1882, was a fiasco, and terribly discouraged Smetana. Fortunately it was followed very shortly by the performance of the completed cycle of tone poems "Má Vlast" which brought him the highest praise accorded to any of his works in his lifetime and erased the memory of his recent disappointment. An enthusiastic demonstration of gratitude to the orchestra of the Prague Opera and the conductor, Adolf Čech, who had taken the initiative in presenting his work, restored to Smetana the confident trust that he was on the threshold of a new period of productivity. In a precarious state of health, he completed the String Quartet in D, his second, intended as a continuation of "From my Life" and therefore also autobiographical. The earlier work, as we know, depicted Smetana's life up to the time that he lost his hearing; the quartet in D concerns his existence as a deaf musician and even, it might be added, as a neurasthenic.

THE NATIONAL THEATRE, PRAGUE

His creative fantasy had been greatly reduced as must be felt in any comparison of the two quartets, nevertheless there are still many deeply sorrowful passages and the mood of resignation and tender reminiscence must move and charm the hearer. Also worthy of mention are the strangely modern harmonizations which, set for example, against the work of such a contemporary as Dvořák, sound almost bizarre.

Although Smetana was aware, as testified by certain articles he wrote for periodicals at that time, "that his activity as a creative artist would soon be over, that slowly the voice of his music would fall silent for ever", he still planned many new compositions and was at work on an opera, "Viola", from Shakespeare's "Twelfth Night", also a cycle for orchestra to be named "Prague Carnival" of which one part, "Introduction and Polonaise", reached completion. Of the opera, there is nothing but 15 pages of score for the orchestra.

There remain a few minor compositions of Smetana's which must be mentioned. In 1878 he wrote the two charming pieces for piano and violin originally known by the German title of "Aus der Heimat" ("From the Fatherland"). Smetana's choral compositions are hardly known outside his own country, one reason being that they were written for Czech texts. The most notable are certainly the ballad for male chorus "Tři Jezdci" ("The Three Horsemen"), of which the Hussite impress on the Czech spirit forms the theme; "Rolnická" ("Peasant's Song"), also for male choir, and "Česká Píseň" ("The Czech Song"), for mixed choir and orchestra, in glorification of the Czech homeland. The "Evening Songs", for piano and voices

(1879), to the words of Hálek, are Smetana's most succesful compositions in this vein.

The life of the master was drawing to its tragic close. A final triumph, such as he had enjoyed at the performance of "Má Vlast", was vouchsafed him when, for the last time, he stood on the podium as a conductor. Shortly before its completion, the National Theatre had been destroyed by fire. From every section of the population came immediate help towards the restoration of this monument to the cultural life of the nation. In aid of the reconstruction of the cultural centre, the orchestra of the National Theatre gave a concert at which Smetana conducted. Aided by the strictest attention of the orchestra he accomplished this practically impossible feat, giving the Overture to "Libuše".

A year after this, in 1882, Smetana was forbidden by his doctors to read for more than fifteen minutes at a time; all musical activities were prohibited. In 1883, when his health for a short period seemed to show some improvement, he worked on his opera "Viola".

On his 60th birthday, March 2nd, 1884, a concert was given in celebration of the event, but his mental state was such that he no longer was fully aware of what was going on about him. On May 12th he died in the National Asylum for the Insane, in Prague and, was buried in the graveyard of Vyšehrad, not far from the city.

Liszt wrote: "In great haste I am writing to tell you what a heavy blow Smetana's death has been to me. He was truly a genius". The art of Liszt was the first great revelation of Smetana's life, and its influence is clear in the three symphonic poems he composed at Göteborg. Wagner was the second great inspiration; but it is remarkable that Smetana's ardent admiration for the master of Bayreuth is not reflected more than passingly in his compositions. Smetana once said, a propos of Wagner's declamatory style and prolonged melodies, "We Czechs are a singing folk; such a means of expression (as Wagner's) is unnatural to us". Also Smetana had no faith in the further development of "absolute music"; on the other hand he interpreted the works of Beethoven, whom he reverenced as a deity, as programme pieces. Of the Romantic musicians, it was Schumann who actually had the most profound influence on his work; that of Chopin is felt only in the delicate virtuosity of his compositions for piano, though, of course, he was famous for his performances of the great Pole's compositions.

The style of Smetana's best work can be regarded as a synthesis of two streams of influence: on one side the two great masters Schumann and Liszt, on the other the great storehouse of Czech folk music. The most perfect examples of his art are "The Bartered Bride," the cycle of tone

30

THE SMETANA MUSEUM, PRAGUE

poems "Má Vlast" and the String Quartet in E, "From my Life". The most distinctive characteristic of his style is a succession of strongly contrasting, often daring, harmonies and rhythms, which yet in no way weakens the direct and simple diatonic nature of the music. The bulk of Smetana's work is unquestionably diatonic, the infrequent use of chromatics occurs only to give point and expression to a passage.

Smetana, blessed with a happy temperament and a serene family life, seemed destined for good fortune; his pride in and high conception of his vocation as an artiste, armed him against the enmity and disappointment commonly encountered by all truly creative spirits. He was borne down at the end of his life, though not without offering the most valiant resistance, by a relentless fate which destroyed him physically and mentally. Smetana's work must be seen as that of a man who faced life with a ready intelligence, a realist with romantic sensitivity, certainly in no way a disturbed or unsubstantial character. The least happy of his compositions are the most emotional, or, the most in conformity with the tastes of his day. The beauty of his epic and lyric evocations of legend and countryside, and his operas — full of dramatic life and, for the greater part, masterly — will, in all probability prove imperishable.

DVOŘÁK'S BIRTHPLACE, NELAHOZEVES (MÜHLHAUSEN)

# ANTONÍN DVOŘÁK

ANTONÍN DVOŘÁK was born on the 8th of September, 1841 in the little village of Nelahozeves, (known under Austrian rule as Mühlhausen) lying on the Moldau some twenty-eight miles north of Prague. His father, František Dvořák, was an innkeeper and butcher who died in 1894, only ten years before his already famous son. His mother, Anna Zdeňka, had been a servant at Lobkowitz castle which dominates the local countryside. These two simple and industrious souls accepted it as their duty to bring up their eight children, of whom the future composer was the oldest, according to their position in society. This meant that when he was eight years old Antonín was sent to the village school so that, after completing the two years of study, which was all that was then required by law, he would be ready to help his parents in their business of the inn.

The school-teacher and organist, Jozef Spitz, was the pride of the community; it was said that he could play on every kind of musical instrument. His pupil studied the violin so assiduously that he was soon able to entertain the visitors at his father's inn and also found himself substituting for his teacher at school. Dvořák used to say in later years that as a boy he had taught music and church singing to every child in Bohemia.

In 1853, the twelve years old boy was sent to live with an uncle in Zlonice, a small town to the west of his native village, where he was to master the German language, then so necessary in business life. The possibility of his becoming a musician had at that time not occurred to any member of his family. The head of the school, the German master and organist, Antonín Liehmann, was here the instrument of Providence. This excellent musician and strict, old-fashioned teacher taught the boy to play the violin, piano and organ and gave him a general grounding in bass viol. His pupil remembered him with gratitude to the end of his days, and portrayed him for posterity as Benda, the schoolmaster-organist in his opera "Jakobín".

Liehmann, who was impressed with the exceptional gifts of young Dvořák, tried with the help of the uncle to persuade the parents that their son deserved the benefit of a proper musical training. But it was not a favourable moment; the Dvořáks had just been forced by financial difficulties to move their business to Zlonice, and the help that Antonín might give about the house was reckoned upon to a greater degree than ever before. In 1854 he was sent to Česká Kamenice in Sudetenland, where his German was to receive a final polishing at a secondary school. Here he found another preceptor in the organist Hancke, under whom he made great strides in organ-playing. Though he now clearly realized that his future must lie in musical pursuits, he was forced against his will and with a bad grace to return the following summer to Zlonice and help his father about the inn. However he was able to continue his studies with Liehmann and finally his uncle Zdeněk came forward with the necessary funds to send him to the School for Organists at Prague. At the same time he had to go on with the study of German; a condition of his coming to Prague had been that he should take lessons from the Franciscans until he had acquired a fluency in the language that would permit him to move at ease anywhere in the old Austrian Empire — which in any case he succeeded in doing, in the course of time.

The School for Organists at Prague, founded by the "Society of Music Lovers" in 1830, was of invaluable service to the generations of Czech composers of that time. The director, Josef Krejčí, a competent teacher, was, though Czech by birth, excessively partial to all things German, including the language. This being Dvořák's weak point, he had great difficulty in doing himself justice with this teacher. His other most important teachers were Fr. Blažek, Josef Foerster (father of the composer Josef Bohuslav

Foerster, dean of the modern Czech School) in organ, and Josef Zvonař. Dvořák also worked steadily as second violinist in the orchestra of "The Society of Saint Cecilia", where, after his classically orientated musical education at the hands of Liehmann, he came to have a thorough knowledge of the works of the early and later romantic masters. One of his fellow-students, Karl Bendl, who made some name for himself as a composer, allowed Dvořák the use of his piano and extensive musical library.

Meanwhile Dvořák's family had moved from Zlonice to Kladno; their worsened financial situation prevented them from giving him any assistance and his uncle also was unable to continue the annual allowance, so the young musician turned to giving lessons as a means of supporting himself. He had at least the good fortune of being able to lodge with another uncle.

In 1859 Dvořák finished the course at the School for Organists. The highest honours went to a student whose name has never been heard of since; Dvořák was content to stand second with the report: "Outstanding talent, particularly in execution; not so strong in theory." The reservation may well have been due to the language difficulty of the pupil and the pro-German bias of Krejčí. In any case when Dvořák did not succeed in finding himself a position as an organist, he took a job as second violinist in the popular concert-orchestra of Karel Momzák, playing night after night in the various places of amusement in Prague. This did not allow him much time to himself; the more remarkable, therefore, is the number of compositions that he completed after 1860.

It was hardly an accident that Dvořák's first composition should be a piece of chamber music; it also gave a clear indication of the road he was to follow as a composer. It had been Smetana's role to give the Czechs a body of national operas; it fell to Dvořák to contribute a store of chamber and orchestral music to the national culture which far outshone anything of that nature that had come before.

This first composition, a string quintet in A minor, was never actually printed. The material of the first and second movements clearly resembles Mozart, the treatment of the 2nd part and Finale — there is no scherzo — is reminiscent of the early Haydn-influenced Beethoven. A year later, in 1862, came a String Quartet in A major Op. 2, which also never appeared in print. At the foot of the last page of the manuscript stand the words "Bohu díky" ("God be thanked") with which every subsequent composition to reach completion was subscribed. This work is in theme and style, even in harmonies and modulations, a tribute to the influence of Schubert. The first motif of the Adagio, the Trio of the Scherzo, and the Finale might well be the work of the Austrian master himself. Nevertheless the Scherzo embodies all the rhythmic elements of the Czech folk dances. All his life Dvořák felt himself much drawn to the music of Beethoven and Schubert. The former he revered as a deity, powerfully attracted by the mighty will and the passionate spirit expressed in the words "Die Musik soll dem Menschen Feuer aus dem Geiste schlagen". ("Music must breathe fire into Man's soul.") While to Schubert's inexhaustible, singing stream of melody he felt an immediate response in the depths of his own nature. Also, like Schubert, Dvořák was not of a contemplative disposition — far less so than Smetana — being, rather, a simple music-maker par excellence.

In his next works the influence of the classic and early romantic masters is also apparent enough, re-worked already into the beginnings of a personal style. A symphony in C minor, "The Bells of Zlonice", dating from 1865, was only discovered in 1923. It is possible that it accidentally escaped the ruthless autos-da-fe to which Dvořák subjected his work during his sixtieth year. The fact that some fragments from this symphony make their appearance in "Silhouettes", Op. 8, for piano, composed in 1879, supports this theory. Unlike two overtures for orchestra, a string quartet, a Mass, a clarinet quartet and a pile of occasional music for theatre programmes, all of which went up in the flames, a symphony in B flat Major and a cello concerto in A Major (which only came to light in 1925 and was then published in a very free version by Günther Raphael) survived. The larger work, though unduly long, contains several passages that presage Dvořák's mature style; the principal subject is full of romantic charm. However the influence of Wagner is by no means foreign to this work, which poses the question of who is most answerable, composer or adaptor, for the final form in which it appeared.

Also never published was the cycle of songs "Cypresses", settings of the poems by G. Pfleger-Moravský, which is a chronicle of Dvořák's fortunes in love. As a music master in the house of the goldsmith Černák he had come to know two of the grown-up daughters: the elder, Josefa, — who became a famous actress and later married a Count Kaunitz — did not return the love he felt for her; but with the second, Anna, a fine altosinger, he was more successful and they were married in 1873. They were blessed with seven children, of whom one, a daughter Ottilie, married Dvořák's pupil Josef Suk, and died only a year after her father. Anna Dvořák outlived her husband by twenty-seven years, dying, in 1931, at the age of seventy-seven.

It must have been on purely personal grounds that Dvořák renamed these pleasantly melodious, but, musically, hardly important songs of the

"Cypresses" cycle "Love-songs", Op. 83 when in 1888 he revised them, and caused him later even to set store on their publication in various forms such as string quartets.

In 1870 Dvořák composed his first opera "Alfred" to a German libretto of Theodore Körner. Of all the forms of composition which he undertook, Dvořák was least successful — in every sense — in his efforts at opera. As opposed to Smetana, whose talents seem to realize themselves more fully in the dramatic form than in his orchestral and chamber music, the intense nature of Dvořák's art rendered it unsuited to the wide musical sphere of opera. The, on the whole, undistinguished and often even trivial music, the over-sweet lyrics and empty pathos of his dramatic works, can bear no comparison with the powers revealed in his chamber music and symphonies. In only one or two of his operas, such as "Jakobín" and "Rusalka" is the original inspiration strong enough to maintain the whole work at a tolerable artistic level throughout. But Dvořák remained in constant touch with operatic and dramatic activities and, during the years that Smetana was conductor at the National Theatre, he played second violin in the orchestra. The influence of the older composer must not, therefore, be underestimated, particularly with respect to the Czech folk music elements which appear in Dvořák's earlier works.

In the libretto of "Alfred" it was surely the theme of national freedom — the opera is concerned with the struggle of the Anglo-Saxons against the Danes in the time of Alfred the Great — which appealed to the composer. But none of this work is ever heard except the Overture, which was published in 1912 under the title "Dramatic" or "Tragic Overture".

Following his first-born in the field of opera — which was never published or performed — Dvořák ventured on a second, "Král a Uhlíř" ("The King and the Charcoalburner"), with a text by B. Guldener. Before this work was completed, a rumour was already in circulation that Antonín Dvořák, a member of the State Theatre Orchestra, had composed a light opera, which was to be produced at the earliest possible moment. But, after a trial, the manuscript was returned to the composer as too difficult, despite Smetana's expressed opinion that it was an artistically-mature work with many inspired passages notwithstanding .With a certain hardy energy characteristic of him, Dvořák re-wrote the entire opera in 1874. While the mark of Wagner's early operas is obvious on "Alfred", the first version of ,,The King and the Charcoalburner" owes much to the early operas of Wagner and uses the idiom of "Die Meistersinger", albeit unobtrusively. In the second version, possibly through his association with Smetana, Dvořák had freed himself from the rather slavish imitation of

Wagner, and the style distinctive of his prime began to proclaim itself — a style combining the elements of the classic and early romantic music with his own romanticism, partly orientated towards Czech folk-lore.

At the same time he had composed several pieces of chamber music, and two string quartets, in D Major and E Minor respectively, in 1870, which were also consigned to the flames, but survive through the fact that copies of the manuscripts were held by his friends. In these two quartets, and in a piano quintet in A Major from 1872, the harmonies are still reminiscent of Wagner. A fragment from the string quartet in E Minor "Andante Religioso", was later revised and became the "Notturno" in B Major Op. 40 for string orchestra. From 1873 dates an also unpublished string quartet in A Minor; a string quartet in F Minor written in the following year was published; its Andante, rewritten as "Romance" for violin and orchestra was published separately, Op. 11. This last makes a somewhat over-orchestrated impression, and the style of the last three parts are "homages" respectively to Mendelssohn, Chopin — in the "Tempo di Valse" — and Schumann. The string quartet in A Minor, Op. 16, written in 1874, is a much more even piece of work, with an Andante full of warmth and feeling; but the spontaneity of the whole work seems hampered by the form adopted. The String Quintet in G Major, with bass viol, Op. 77, which was written in the following year (1875) makes by contrast a strange impression. It must be remarked in passing that the opus numbers attached to Dvořák's works are of absolutely no chronological significance. It was largely the publisher, Simrock, who when he purchased a composition which Dvořák may have had lying completed for years, gave it for the sake of convenience an opus number according to the order of publication. This is illustrated by the fact that a string quartet in E Major composed in 1876, was numbered Op. 80; the famous Piano Quintet in A Major written in 1887 numbered Op. 81; and the already mentioned "Love Songs", a revision of work composed in 1865, Op. 83.

This String Quartet Op. 77, if compared with a piece dating from Dvořák's best period is certainly quite out of harmony as far as style is concerned, even as a youthful product it is disappointing enough. Its utter lack of melodic charm places it among Dvořák's least successful works.

The two Trios and the Piano Quartet written at the same time, are a noted advance. The Adagio molto e mesto in G Minor from the first Trio in B Major Op. 21, has already the Slavonic, faintly melancholic colouring, characteristic of Dvořák's mature style. This colouring or mood of music was often referred to as "Dumka" by the composer, a word of European Russian derivation which is applied to elegiac poetry or ballads. Through

Dvořák's use of the term, "Dumka" has become a generally familiar expression for a Slavonic melody, usually in a minor key, in slow 2/4 time, in the course of which a major passage almost always occurs. The Dumka may stand as a piece in its own right or may be part of a larger composition. The second trio in G Minor Op. 26, lacks the fresh naturalness of the first, and is somewhat spoiled by the finale in which the musical elements are strung together without being fully realized. The Piano Quartet in D Major Op. 23, is certainly not very important, or original, but the technical treatment foreshadows that of Dvořák's fully developed style, with such features as his partiality for the contrast of two beat and three beat rhythms, either simultaneously or following on each other, or carried by different instruments. The piano part in the finale of this work is, for instance, in 6/8 time, while that of the strings is in 2/4, or the other way round.

Immediately after finishing the Trio in G Minor, Dvořák started work on a string quartet in E Major Op. 80.(1) This work, which string ensembles hardly ever perform, should be much more frequently heard, if only for the magnificent Andante con moto. The quiet Slavonic melancholy which pervades this piece makes it one of the outstanding early works of the composer. The combination of the first and the second theme by the first violin and violincello is a singularly attractive feature.

Meanwhile, Dvořák had also been occupied in symphonic composition. From the years 1873/1874 date two symphonies, in E Major and D Minor. Smetana conducted the symphony in E Major in Prague in 1874 but it was only published in 1912, with no opus number attached. The composer retained a particular affection for this work to the end of his life, although it had very little originality and sounded as much like Wagner as Dvořák. The reason for this predilection had very probably nothing to do with its musical value. Dvořák had submitted it to the Commission for the National Music Award in Vienna, the judges being the famous (and equally notorious) aesthete and critic, Eduard Hanslick — who detested Wagner, Bruckner and Wolff and was an apostle of Brahms — Johann Herbeck, conductor of the Viennese State Opera, and the object of Hanslick's adoration, Johannes Brahms himself. All three recognised the strong and original talent of Dvořák, and as a primary result he won the State Award in 1873 and for several subsequent years; the second and no less important result was the lifelong friendship that grew up between Brahms and the young Czech composer, eight years his junior.

The government stipend was a great help in his straightened circumstances to Dvořák who, in order to be able to devote the evenings to composi-

38

tion, had resigned his position as second violinist at the Opera becoming organist at the church of Saint Adalbert, though he thus earned less than before.

"The Moravian Duets" Op. 32, were also profitable for Dvořák. Brahms was so taken with these songs that he sent an enthusiastic letter to his publisher, Simrock, and thus secured their publication under the title, "Klänge aus Mähren". From then on, Simrock became the publisher of the Czech master and, except for a few more or less accidental interruptions, brought out the greater part of his work.

Although Dvořák and Brahms were close friends, Dvořák's great admiration for the German composer had remarkably little effect on his own composition. Immediately after he made Brahms' acquaintance, his style, especially in his chamber music, underwent some passing influence by the latter, an example being the beautiful String Quintet in A Major Op. 48. In general, however, Dvořák's apparent derivation from Brahms is rather a result of their very similar musical grounding, based as it was on the classical masters (particularly Beethoven), and Schubert, though Brahms was also influenced by Bach and his predecessors, who have left clear traces in his compositions; an essential element of Dvořák's work, on the other hand, was his close affinity in rhythm and melody with Czech and other Slavonic folk music.

The solitary North-German Protestant, Brahms, like Bruckner and Beethoven a lifelong bachelor, from whom his friends had to endure the queer moroseness behind which he masked his sensitive and vulnerable nature, was in almost every respect, a complete contrast to his young friend, a Czech, a Catholic, a happily married man with a growing family, and, finally, an uncomplicated character without any psychological conflicts. It is remarkable that their esteem and regard for each other seems to have remained undiminished throughout the long years of their association. Of course Dvořák was allied to Brahms in belonging to the "absolute music" school of thought, and his innumerable symphonic and chamber music works were ammunition in the battle against the hateful theories of Wagner and Liszt. The "Five Symphonic Poems", which Dvořák composed in the last year of his life, must therefore have been offensive to Brahms, but their personal friendship does not seem to have suffered.

Like Smetana, Dvořák was an optimist, but he was spared the terrible blows of fate against which the former had to struggle so long and so heroically. Despite the fame he achieved, Dvořák remained all his life a simple man; his most striking characteristics were a childlike credulity, a great attachment to his family, and a truly remarkable taciturnity. His rural

THE DVOŘÁK MUSEUM, PRAGUE

origin had given him a familiarity with and a deeply rooted love for nature. This feeling was demonstrated in the pastoral parts of his work which are very often the most beautiful passages in the symphonies and chamber music.

Dvořák made his home in Prague, where he lived until his death. From 1884 onwards he spent the summer at his country home at Vysoká. His two journeys to America in the years 1892/1895, his visits to England and his concert tours, were only great and small interruptions in a very regular way of life. By 1876 his financial situation was so much improved that he could resign his post of organist. The following year he moved to a larger house in the Žitná Ulice, near what was then known as the Franz Jozef Station. Here he was fascinated to an increasing degree by the locomotives. He considered them as the greatest of technical miracles and even tried to learn by heart the numbers of the engines and the names of the engine-drivers. Josef Suk had an amusing story about this curious hobby: during his engagement to Ottilie, one of Dvořák's daughters, he once proudly informed his future father-in-law that he had noted the number of the engine of the train on which he had travelled. Dvořák replied testily that the locomotive could not possibly have had that number, that it must have been the tender, and, turning, to his daughter with a simulated reproach in his voice, he said to her, "And this is the man you want to marry!"

40

Another anecdote concerns his taciturnity. When Dvořák and the poet Vrchlický were travelling to Vienna to take their seats as members of the Austrian "Herrenhaus", they passed through a swampy region where Vrchlický expressed his wonder at the clouds of mosquitos. Dvořák did not make any remark until they were walking down the Ringstrasse in Vienna; then he observed: "I suppose the water attracts them."

Dvořák's political activities were limited to this one session. He took the oath

ANTONÍN DVOŘÁK (1901)

and voted in favour of the passage of the law under discussion and then left the Herrenhaus for ever. As a momento, he brought home some well-sharpened pencils he had found on his desk, which, as he told his wife, would serve him well in his musical work.

Before coming to Dvořák's compositions, we must say something about the order of his symphonies to clear up the general confusion brought about by their numbering. Until a short while ago, the well known symphony in E Minor entitled "From the New World", was the only one played in this country. It is called the Fifth but is in fact the Ninth. Here follows a list, in chronological order, of Dvořák's last five symphonies:

Fifth symphony, known as the Third, in F Major originally Op. 24 later
Op. 76, 1875

Sixth symphony, known as the First, in D Major, op. 60, 1880.
Seventh symphony, known as the Second, in D Minor op. 70, 1884—1885
Eighth symphony, known as the Fourth, in G Major op. 88, 1889
Ninth symphony known as the Fifth, (New World Symphony) in E Minor
Op. 95, 1893

We now come to the years of Dvořák's maturity as a composer, say from 1875 until his first visit to the United States in 1892. The works of the time before may be considered as products of his period of development; those composed later fail, with a few happy exceptions, to reach the heights

41

achieved in the symphonies listed above. Owing to lack of space, it is impossible to give a chronological table of the large body of work that Dvořák produced in less than thirty years, from 1872 until his death in 1904. His crowning musical achievements were, in the first, chamber music, and then his symphonic creations; the choral works, with some reservations, take the next place. His "Stabat Mater" and "Te Deum" must be counted among the best of Dvořák's compositions, while the "Requiem" is a beautiful although not such a completely satisfactory work. However, Dvořák's deepest and most individual self is undeniably represented in the more intense and compact music of his symphonies and works for chamber orchestra.

To begin with these latter, the String Quartet in D Minor Op. 34, 1877, dedicated to Brahms, much resembles the work of Schubert in one of his melancholy, melodious moods. Nevertheless, the Adagio, in 3/4 time, has already that stately lyricism which is characteristic of the slow movements of Dvořák's chamber music and also of some of his symphonies. The "con sordino" of the strings imparts a peculiar attraction to this piece. An important step towards a more clearly defined, individual style is the subsequent String Quartet in E flat Major Op. 51. 1879. Dvořák's most pronouncedly Slavonic compositions belong in the main, to this middle period. The splendid Dumka in G Minor, andante con moto, (with a vivace in G Major in 3/4 time on the pattern of a Furiant, as intermezzo) is an outstanding example of Dvořák's style in this respect, and typical of the works he composed in the eighties. The String Quartet in C Major, Op. 61, has, as a whole, less spontaneity and imagination. It might be suggested that this work is more the product of a perfected technique than of genuine inspiration, were it not for the poco adagio in F Major, in 4/4 time, one of the most delicately sensitive pieces of music Dvořák ever wrote. The stylistic affinity with the work of Schumann is rather marked, but the fact that it is an arrangement of the original slow movement of the violin sonata Op. 57, explains the fact that the accompaniment might have been written for piano. The Sextet for Strings in A Major Op. 48, with its opulently beautiful tone, was the special favourite of Brahms and is reminiscent in its lyrical spontaneity and freshness, of the early chamber music work of the master, and shares with it characteristics derived from Schubert. The Trio for violin, cello and piano in F Minor Op. 65, the magnificent Piano Quintet in A Major Op. 81 and the last two String Quartets, are Dvořák's opera magna in the field of chamber music. The sincerity and torment of the Trio are manifest in the choice of the dramatic F Minor, in which key Beethoven's "Egmont Overture", the "Appassionata", and the

MANUSCRIPT OF THE OPENING BARS OF STRING QUARTET OP. 51

piano quintets of Brahms and Franck were written. In style and outer form, it bears much resemblance to the work of Brahms, but the overwhelming inner suspense and passionate fervour are the pure expression of Dvořák's distinctive genius. None of his other great compositions surpassed this work which must certainly be termed a masterpiece. The powerful, soaring passages of the third movement poco adagio in A Major, in 4/4 time, interposed in the part in B Major, belong to Dvořáks' most expressive moments, full of distinctive beauty of melody and harmony. The famous Piano Quintet in A Major Op. 81, to be classed with those of Schumann, Brahms and Franck, entirely lacks the unusual darkly dramatic atmosphere of the Trio. It is an extraordinarily satisfying work, in the best romantic tradition, a delight to the educated musician and the simplest listener alike. The magnificent fortissimo climax of the first movement, where the subject is borne irresistibly onward by piano and strings, the masterly Dumka in F Minor, in the form of a rondo, and, in short, the perfection and balance of the splendid work, justify the fame it enjoys.

43

The Piano Quartet in E Major Op. 87, 1889, granted its wealth of attention to detail, evokes a slightly sceptical attitude. The direct expressiveness of the preceding work here seems to be replaced by a not wholly agreeable echo of virtuosity and melodramatic colouring. The lyrical passages in G Major in the slow movement, are pleasing but almost too sweet. However there are, even so, many excellent passages and some of the modulations are examples of Dvořák's ingenuity at its best.

The Trio, Op. 90, 1890—1891, in construction rather resembling a rhapsody, consists of six parts, each of them representing a dumka, and Dvořák gave it the name of "Dumky", the plural of dumka. This brilliant work in which score and instruments are so happily matched, equals if not surpasses, the Piano Quintet. The alternating fast and slow tempo of each part, typical of the dumka, gives the structure a certain monotony perhaps, but the free play of the imagination which inspires the whole, saves it from any sense of limitation imposed by the form.

To mention Dvořák's minor chamber music, one of the pieces most worthy of note is Op. 47, written for the curious combination of two violins, cello and harmonium (or piano).

It is an admirable piece of intimate music, although the piano is a poor substitute for the peculiar harmonium-tone, derived from the smooth continuity of chords. Its name, "Maličkosti" ("Bagatelles") can be taken in the sense Beethoven gave to it. The charming Trio in C Major Op. 74, is an excellent piece for the domestic circle, at least in the hands of competent performers. The thema con variazioni is a little gem, full of expression and rich dynamic variation. The "Romantic Pieces" for violin and piano, Op. 75, also written in 1887, are straightforward and pleasant without any particular pretentions. The Violin Sonata in F Major, Op. 58, is a stepchild of Dvořák's muse; it might as well have been written by any German follower of the schools of Schumann and Brahms. Despite its spirited rhythm, the finale is of no real consequence. The Sonatina, written during his American period, is Dvořák's only work for violin and piano of any importance.

Dvořák's Fourth Symphony in G Major, Op. 88 (actually the eighth), written in 1889, shows him at his symphonic best and is, at the same time, his most individual evocation of the spirit and nature of his Czech homeland. Smetana's comparable work, "Má Vlast" was more objective in approach and took an epic form; with Dvořák the lyrical, subjective impulse predominates. While the New World Symphony leaped into popularity immediately after its first performance, becoming Dvořák's best known work for full orchestra, it is only in the last ten years that this uncommonly complete and poetic symphony in G Major has taken its merited place in the repertoires of symphony orchestras.

The sonata form, which Dvořák had followed rather consistently in his previous symphonies, is here observed only in a most general way. The thematic profusion is truly astonishing, and it is a tribute to the ingenuity with which the composer juxtaposes melodies in fascinating contrasts that the listener does not feel overwhelmed. The moving lyrical passages in G Major, 4/4 time and in the Adagio in C Minor, 2/4 time, make it one of the most beautiful slow movements of symphonic literature. In the second subject, in C Major, of this Adagio, with an accompaniment in sixths, strongly reminiscent of Bruckner, the exquisite thematic material is exploited to the uttermost; the following allegretto grazioso, and the finale, Allegro ma non troppo, in G Major, 2/4 time, are less intensely developed, though this latter part, a veiled "theme with variations", has an interesting treatment, and with the tenderly romantic coda, contains passages of high quality and beauty. The blooming, colourful orchestral dress of the symphony, the complete spontaneity and naturalness of the design underlying the finished surface, made for this symphony a host of friends — when it finally became known.

The three symphonies which immediately preceded this great one in G, have now, broadly speaking, lost something of their importance. The earliest is the symphony in F Major, Op. 76, known as the Third. Apart from the poetic and pastoral opening of the first movement and a charming, melancholy Andante con moto, it contains enough agreeable and even excellent and beautiful touches, but cannot as a whole be considered as very noteworthy.

Whenever Dvořák, overstepping the limitations of his great and even inspired talent, strove to reach beyond the natural ardour and deep sincerity of his particular genius into the sphere of the grandly impressive and tragic, a composition resulted which falls irrevocably into the class of what are generally called imitations. The Second Symphony in D Minor, Op. 70, 1884—1885, actually the Seventh, is a clear case of this kind, while its predecessor, the First Symphony in D Major, Op. 60, 1880, actually the Sixth, the most "Slavonic" of the last five, is very much less forced and therefore more sincere. The principal themes of the first and last movements are so much like those of Brahms' Second Symphony in the same key, that, were there not certain passages wholly typical of Dvořák, the term plagiarism would be justified. It must be said that the slow movements of both symphonies are among the most successful passages of the composer. The Adagio from Op. 60 is reminiscent of the Adagio of Beethoven's Ninth —

both are in B flat Major — but soon passes on to a warm lyrical passage, filled with a sunny and pastoral atmosphere. The theme of the Poco adagio in F Major, 4/4 time, must be recognised as filled with some of Dvořák's deepest and most genuine inspiration. Beginning with a passage of perfect classic repose the principal subject develops an unexpectedly intense, yet delicate, emotion before the onset of the beautiful coda. Dvořák seldom surpassed such heights of inspiration in his symphonies. The tragic atmosphere is not sustained throughout as it is, for instance, in the compelling First Symphony of Brahms, which it resembles in mood, or in the First Piano Concerto of the same composer, where form and idea are of a comparable grandeur.

The disappointment which must be caused by such pieces of music as the first and last movements of the Symphony in D Major seem to arise from their inadequate spiritual content. Dvořák was no less capable of deep reflection on the problems of his work than Brahms, but the latter, with his melancholy, resigned temperament, explored the dark places of his soul and reached a much more profound habit of expression, either in proud rebellion or, especially later, in sad acquiescence. Dvořák escaped — and was assuredly personally the happier therefore — the visitations of demons which have made many of the great suffer deeply; hence his less universal personality as evinced in his work. His healthy and upright temperament enabled him, on the other hand, to express his warm and intense inner life without falling into psychological complications, and to be faithful to his genius in a way only possible to a simple composer such as he remained all his life.

The Violin Concerto in A Minor, Op. 53, 1879—1880, may not be one of the great concertos of the nineteenth century but, compared to the popular and still much played Violin Concerto in G by Max Bruch, for instance, it is a classic. It is certainly not a work of genius such as the Cello Concerto of a much later date, but the Adagio ma non troppo in F Major, 3/8 time, is inspired to a lyrical outpouring which gives the soloist the opportunity to develop an absolutely pure cantabile, and with respect to this movement, it is one of Dvořák's outstanding concertos. The Finale, a furiant with a dumka as middle passage, contains all the charm of the Czech national melody and rhythm.

Dvořák also composed a series of shorter works for orchestra, one of the very best of which is "Symphonic Variations" Op. 78, 1877, almost unknown in this country. The theme is an adaptation of a chorus for male voices, from the opera "Guslar" ("The Violinist") of the same year. The masterly variations on this utterly simple though expressive theme, display such a store of moods and transformations, of admirable tone-figures and melodic touches, that it is regrettable indeed that a work of such ingenuity and inexhaustible creative power is neglected in concert programmes in favour of mediocre compositions such as the "Slavonic Rhapsodies", Op. 45. Here there is a vague and occasional reference to the grandezza of Czech folk music, but the main impression must be that everything has been sacrificed to please the popular taste. A graceful and very sympathetic work is the "Scherzo Capricioso" Op. 66, 1883, which, in the waltz passages produces an atmosphere remarkably resembling that of Richard Strauss's youthful "Burlesque" for piano and orchestra; the Pococo tranquillo has a curious suggestion of Bruckner. This "Dance Rhapsody" has a much more universal appeal than the justly famous "Slavonic Dances", the title of which work offended the fiery nationalist Smetana, who had expressly called his corresponding composition "Czech Dances". Dvořák did not for that matter limit himself strictly to the dances of his own country — the second part of this work, dating from 1886, contains compositions based on dances from other Slav countries such as Serbia, Ukraine, Moravia, and Poland. Both the first of the series, (Op. 46) written in 1878, and the second, Op. 72, were originally conceived for piano with four hands, but the composer rearranged them immediately for orchestra — in which instrumental setting their colourful beauty is realized to the fullest advantage. The melodies and rhythms, now smiling and sad, now stately and majestic, and the lovely contrasts, make these "Slavonic Dances" a work of high artistic level, yet approachable for all.

Dvořák had at one time planned to write three overtures with the collective title "Nature, Love and Life"; later he called them separately "V přírodé", ("In Nature") Op. 91, "Carnival", Op. 92 and "Othello" Op. 93, 1891. These overtures are variations on a central theme of a pastoral character, and are an indication of the direction which his "Five Symphonic Poems", his last work for orchestra, was to take. The most successful, though somewhat monotonous is "In Nature", which is filled with a sense of open air and light; "Carnival", except for the middle episode with the appearance of the principal motif, is a rather ordinary and somewhat noisy composition. "Othello" is better realized, but expresses more the demonic struggle between love and jealousy than the tragedy of Shakespeare's play.

The "Husitská" ("Hussite Overture"), 1883, is little more than a thorough exploitation of the chorals "Kdož jsú Boží Bojovníci" and "Svatý Václave"; however it is an imposing work filled with intense feeling.

Among Dvořák's lighter compositions for orchestra must be mentioned the "Serenade for String Orchestra" in A Major Op. 22, written in 1875, with its fine brief Larghetto, and the Serenade in D Minor, Op. 44, 1878, for woodwind, cello and bass viol, a happy example of an adaptation of the eighteenth century cassation. The "Česká Suita" ("Czech Suite") in D Major, Op. 39, written in 1879, is clearly affected by the first part of the Slavonic Dances which Dvořák had just brought to completion. The opening "Pastorale" is most rightly named and sings a pastoral air to the accompaniment of a bagpipe bass.

As has been mentioned already, Dvořák composed a number of important works for choir. The earliest, the "Stabat Mater", Op. 58 (1876/77). an ambitious work for solo voices, choir, orchestra and organ, has a more lyrical-meditative than epic-dramatic character. The respected position it occupies in the body of music for choirs is due more to the deep sincerity and emotion of the withal unequal music than to the grandiose conception inspired by the text. The fact that Dvořák was not particularly sensitive to the mood of the text he chose — a very obvious fault in his songs — is apparent here, but on the whole the composition maintains a level worthy of the subject matter, though the excessive chromatic transitions in the first chorus disturb the ear.

The "Requiem" Op. 89, 1890, for solo voices, choir and orchestra is also a work of considerable importance. The principal motif, which recurs throughout, is based on the Introit of the Gregorian Requiem Mass. Dvořák manages to heighten the dramatic suspense and to give a variety to the music by an alternation of choir and soloists in the successive parts, which are bound into a unity by the tragic and moving melody of the leading motif. The "Stabat Mater" and the "Requiem" have achieved considerable popularity, particularly in England.

The Mass in D Major Op. 86, 1887, is a work about which there is not much (either good or bad) to be said; it is church music of a conventional nature, containing a few passages which can compel attention. The oratorium "Svatá Ludmila" Op. 71, 1885—1886, based on a text by the prominent Czech poet Jaroslav Vrchlický, intended for performance in England, is in three parts, the first of which paints a pagan feast and is musically the most interesting on account of its freshness of tone and idea; the two last, however, are the type of music usually heard at the performances of music clubs.

As for the operas, a type of composition in which Dvořák obstinately persevered, though without any reward either of outer success or inner satisfaction, the best that can be said of them is that it might perhaps be worth while to orchestrate for concert performance excerpts from the best

48

**DAYS WITH CELEBRITIES (221).**
DVORAK.

49

parts of "Král a Uhlíř" ("The King and the Charcoalburner"), 1871, "Tvrdé palice" ("The Stubborn Peasants") 1874, and "Šelma Sedlák" ("The Scoundrelly Peasant"), 1877. In 1882 Dvořák undertook the composition of a new dramatic opera "Dimitry" Op. 64, based on a text of Maria Rieger Červinka, which is a sequel to Moussorgsky's "Boris Godunov". It can be readily understood that this work enjoyed only a very moderate success when it was presented at the Prague Opera in Vienna following on the "Bartered Bride" of Smetana. The public could not but be aware of the vast difference in quality between the latter and Dvořák's far from original offering, which is, in fact, little more than a superficial emulation of Wagner mixed with a rich tribute to the work of Meyerbeer. Dvořák's next opera "Jakobín" ("The Jacobin") Op. 84, 1887—1888, also on a text by Maria Rieger Červinka, deserved a better fate than it met. Set in the time of the French Revolution, the action takes place in the castle of a nobleman and later in a small Bohemian village. Dvořák, with his country upbringing, treated both setting and story — a tale of faithful lovers beset by every kind of malicious intrigue and danger, which they duly overcome to reach a happy ending — with great sympathy, making of it an opportunity to express his own romantic temperament. The score is filled with a lyrical tenderness, humour and colour. A character which he handles with particular affection is that of Benda, the old-fashioned music master, a portrait full of delicately humorous touches of his old teacher Liehmann.

The creative period discussed above can be regarded as coming to an end with Dvořák's fiftieth birthday, which he celebrated in 1881. His dislike of public demonstrations caused him, world famous as he was beginning to be, to keep himself as much as possible in the background on this occasion.

Since that time when, through the intervention of Brahms, the Berlin publisher Simrock had begun to bring out his works, Dvořák had been financially independent, and able to devote himself without interruption to composition. Most of his time was indeed given to work; the dates of inception and completion of a piece, usually to be found on his manuscript, make it evident that he seldom took more than a day's rest before starting a new composition. When Brahms in the eighties tried to persuade Dvořák to settle in Vienna, the latter found for excuse the fact that his children spoke only Czech; but the truth of the matter was that he firmly desired to live his own life, both as a Czech and as a composer. Dvořák made his first trip to England in 1884; it was a sort of triumphal tour. Between 1884 and 1890 he visited that country six times, and in the following year he received a great honour, the degree D. Mus. Honoris Causa, from the University of Cambridge.

Mrs Jeannette Thurber, founder of the National Conservatory of New York, a private music school, discovered in Dvořák precisely the proper musical personage to draw attention to the Conservatory and invited him to fill the position of director. After an initial refusal, Dvořák accepted this financially very attractive offer. For his farewell trip through Czechoslovakia, which he made in the company of the violinist Lachner and the cellist Hanuš Wihan, later of the Bohemian String Quartet, he composed the beautiful Rondo in G Minor, Op. 94, for cello and piano, later re-written for full orchestra.

In September Dvořák left Prague taking with him his wife, two of his children and a young man, called Kavařík, a student at the Prague Conservatoire; the party reached New York within the month. In the course of the many agreeable activities of his stay in the New World, Dvořák made himself thoroughly acquainted with the music of the American negroes, which came about partly through his contact with negro students at the Conservatoire. He studied in particular the spirituals, now considered so interesting in Europe, and the everyday plantation songs of the former slaves. An unusual characteristic of this music is the pentatonic scale, that is to say, our scale, lacking the fourth and the seventh notes. Also typical are the syncopated and punctuated rhythms, and, further, in the minor key the seventh note of the scale is lowered and the sixth omitted.

For the celebration in 1892 of the fourth centenary of the discovery of America, Dvořák had composed the "Te Deum", Op. 103 while still at his country house at Vysoká. This is his last important choral work, and, in its compact brevity, probably his finest. The opening recalls Bach; the development in G Major, 4/4 time, is filled with a radiant faith and joy. The work falls into parts on the plan of a symphony, having both a slow movement and a scherzo. The great subtlety of the choral and orchestral details and the excellent musical quality of the whole, places this composition among Dvořák's best.

In New York Dvořák tried to live, in as far as possible, as he had at home, with all the daily habits and hobbies peculiar to him. He soon found his way to the railway stations and took a train ride of an hour outside New York in order to see the Chicago express dash past at full speed. When the station officials began to find his inquisitiveness annoying he betook himself to the docks where, since at sailing time visitors were allowed aboard, he was able to study the ships (inside and out) to his heart's content.

MANUSCRIPT OF THE OPENING BARS OF THE LARGO OF THE NEW WORLD SYMPHONY

His musical duties at the Conservatory consisted of giving three lessons and directing two orchestral performances a week. Longfellow's "Song of Hiawatha" aroused his interest, as he noted in his journal, and his "Legende," written in December 1892, on this subject, contains the motif which he used as the central theme of the Largo of the New World Symphony.

The symphony itself was brought to completion in May 1893 in New York, and thereupon Dvořák altered his arrangements — he had planned to return to Czechoslovakia in the summer — and decided to visit Kavařic, at Spillville in Iowa, instead. He telegraphed his four older children to join him and in July the whole family set off for Spillville, a small town at that time mainly inhabited by Czech immigrants. This factor, and the complete quiet of the surroundings probably account for the fact that Dvořák found himself much happier there than in the cosmopolitan New York. Every morning he played the organ at the church and in a very short time the town people had begun to idolize their famous compatriot.

Meanwhile Simrock was printing the new symphony and Brahms further showed his friendship by undertaking to correct the proofs — which

52

he subsequently did for all the compositions of Dvořák's time in the United States. As Dvořák wrote to Simrock: "I can hardly believe that there is another composer in the world who would do as much".

The "Z nového světa" ("The New World Symphony") in E Minor, Op. 95, was Dvořák's last and ninth symphony: this magical number seems not to have been without influence. Known as the Fifth, it is by far the most popular of Dvořák's works for full orchestra. Like the Fifth and Sixth symphonies of Tschaikovsky, it owes its immense

THE BOHEMIAN STRING QUARTET (1893)

success to its musical intelligibility and its romanticism, often bordering on sentimentality. But these features cannot obscure its real and considerable virtues. The instrumentation is masterly with its full romantic phrasing and orchestral opulence. The American influence produces a certain dualism; Dvořák wrote to the conductor Oscar Nedbal, who was to conduct a performance in Berlin, "Do not let the nonsense that I have made use of original American melodies appear on the programme."

These "original American melodies" were the negro spirituals already mentioned, and the fact that Dvořák had indeed given the work a certain local colour somewhat contradicts his statement above. However, the Americanisms, a few themes adapted from spirituals in a dull and featureless European manner, are certainly the least successful parts of the work. Also the use of sequences in the opening and closing movements is perhaps lavish and even the great pace and sweep of these allegro passages hardly entitles them to be classed with the finest of Dvořáks's symphonic inspirations. But where, on the other hand, the composer sings, in his distinctive accents, of the noble, melancholy solitude of nature, and of his longing for his Bohemian homeland, the hearer is unable to resist the emotion with which the clear and unhesitating voice fills him.

While at Spillville, Dvořák composed the famous String Quartet in

53

F Major, Op. 96, 1893, also redolent of the voices of nature but of a more lyrical mood, except for the nostalgic lento in D Minor in 6/8 time. This is one of his most intensely felt and expressed works. The String Quintet in E flat, Op. 97, was also written in these country surroundings. The Larghetto con varizioni in C Major, is the crowning point of this composition which, like the preceding one, is full of the voices of nature. The peculiar rhythms of the Scherzo were, it seems, suggested by the music and dances of the Iroquois Indians with which Dvořák had become acquainted at Spillville.

Dvořák returned to New York, where he stayed until early in 1894. His second journey to America took place between the autumn of that year and April of 1895. The most important work of his second visit was the Cello Concerto in B Minor, Op. 104, which, rightly, is highly esteemed by all cellists. The score is really quite exceptional in the happy compatibility of inspiration and solo instrument. The first movement, Allegro in 4/4 time, is constructed like that of a sonata but without the elaboration. One of the most lovely episodes is that in G Minor with the fine flute counterpart. The thematically rich Adagio ma non troppo in G Major, 3/4 time, in which the air "Kéž duch můj sám" ("Let Me Be") from Op. 82 is recalled, and the Rondo finale in B Minor, 2/4 time, which commences as a Slav march and comes to a close with a tenderly poetic epilogue, maintain the high level of inspiration.

Even the energetic and businesslike Mrs Thurber was not able to persuade Dvořák to make his home in the United States. High honours, such as the honorary membership of the Philharmonic Society, notwithstanding, Dvořák held fast to his resolve to return home. His last composition on American soil was a part of the opening of the String Quartet in A flat Major, which was completed only in the autumn in Prague, where the master had resumed his lessons at the Conservatoire. This Quartet in A flat Major, Op. 105, and the Quartet in G Major Op. 106, 1895, are the most perfect of his chambermusic works; they were also his last compositions to be classed as "pure music". Of the two, the Quartet in A flat is the less complicated. The delicately balanced Scherzo indicates a trend — always apparent in this movement with Dvořák — towards an aetherialized rhythm. The most moving passage is certainly the sublime Adagio in F Major, 4/4 time; here the pastoral song of praise generally embodied in the best of Dvořák's slow movements, swells to a veritable hymn, and there is throughout a spiritual discipline which the master was not always so successful in attaining. The second quartet is technically still more elaborate, with an unusually complicated imitative arrangement

FROM THE FIRST MOVEMENT OF THE CELLO CONCERTO OP. 104

and a profundity and sincerity of emotion which set this String Quartet in G Major among the best works of the kind since the masterpieces of Beethoven. Indeed the first part, the Adagio in E Major, 3/8 time, realizes the ideal towards which Dvořák had always striven with all his powers. In none of the few works which he produced in the following years did he reach such heights.

In 1895 and 1896 Dvořák abruptly turned to the symphonic poem as a means of expression. This conversion may be partially accounted for by the contact he had had in New York with the conductor Anton Seidl, a fiery partisan of Wagner and Liszt. In any case, and whatever may have

OPENING BARS OF THE SECOND MOVEMENT OF THE STRING QUARTET OP. 105

been the causes, while in America the hidden ties which had bound Dvořák to his revered friend and colleague Brahms were loosened. Dvořák was no theoretician; his impulses were emotional and he did not follow any reasoned principle in this matter. His five Symphonic Poems in chronological order were:

"Vodník", ("The Watercarrier"), Op. 107, "Polednice", ("The Noon Witch") Op. 108; "Zlatý Kolovrat", ("The Golden Spinning wheel") Op. 109; "Holovbek", ("The Woodpigeon") Op. 110, and "Píseň bohatýrská", ("The Hero's Song") Op. 111. The stories which inspired most of them came from the collection "Ballads and Fairytales" of K. J. Erben, mentioned before.

It would take too long to tell the involved and often weird stories of these pieces. As music they are not particularly distinguished, but the great freshness and colourfulness and the little refinements in orchestration make them very pleasant to listen to. In his anxiety to remain faithful to his text Dvořák seems to have sacrificed much of his usual spontaneity.

The light opera "Čert a Káča" ("The Devil and Catharina") Op. 112,

A PASSAGE FROM THE SECOND MOVEMENT OF THE STRING QUARTET OP. 105

composed in 1898—1899 to a text of Adolf Wenzig was, for Dvořák, a success. The setting is partly on earth, partly in hell; the devil is thoroughly bam-
boozled by the dauntless heroine Catharina, whose happy fate is assured
in the end. After enjoying a short spell of popularity this opera vanished
for ever from the regular repertoires, though in 1932 it made a fleeting
reappearance when it was put on by the Oxford University Opera Club.
The only operatic work of Dvořák which has maintained its popularity,
and that in a degree only second to Smetana's much-loved "Bartered
Bride" is "Rusalka" Op. 114, composed in 1900 to a text of Jaroslav
Kvapil. The story is the ancient Germanic legend of Undine, which so
attracted the early Romantics. The fairy-tale atmosphere of the music
reflects the influence of Wagner's chromatically-flavoured style and while
there are many excellent passages, the rather stereotyped fantasy and
disturbing sentimentality — always unfortunately present in Dvořák's

57

A SCENE FROM THE OPERA "ARMIDA"

operas, — cannot be ignored. Nevertheless from a technical and instrumental viewpoint, this is his most attractive operatic work.

Dvořák's last opera and his last completed composition was "Armida" Op. 115, composed in 1902—1903, to a libretto by Jaroslav Vrchlický, based on an excerpt from Tasso's "Gerusalemme Liberata". It is an example of the worst operatic tradition in the style of Meyerbeer and the Italian Verists.

The most delightful work of this, Dvořák's last period of creative activity, was the minor but admirable Sonatina for Violin and Piano in G. Major Op. 100, written in 1893 for his children, and for which he himself always felt a great fondness. It is ideal for the drawing-room, with no further claims than to present the domestic performer with a piece of music of genuine artistic worth. The short Larghetto in G Minor, 2/4 time, is based on a theme inspired by the sight of the Minnehaha waterfall and is the most noteworthy passage of the work. Dvořák's piano-music as a whole hardly needs to be reviewed in detail. The most important examples are the "Theme and Variations" Op. 36, and the "Humoresques" Op. 101, among which latter is the famous "Humoresque in G Major".

Of his Duets the works which must be mentioned are the "Slavonic Dances", "Legendes", Op. 59; "From the Bohemian Forests", Op. 68,

58

and "Poetic Moods", Op. 85, all of which have their attractive points. The best solo songs to piano accompaniment are the "Gypsy Melodies", Op. 55, for which there is also an orchestral accompaniment, and the "Bible Songs", Op. 99. The music of these latter is only barely related to the imposing text and illustrates them in a conventional and extremely simple fashion. The best two-part works for voice are the "Moravian Duets", Op. 32. Lastly the Piano Concerto in G Minor, Op. 39, must be listed, though hardly on account of any particularly outstanding qualities, nor the skilful use of the solo instrument.

Dvořák's last years passed quietly without any occurrences of great importance. His sixtieth birthday in 1901 was the occasion of a tremendous celebration. He was elected member of the "Herrenhaus" and made director of the Conservatoire, though he left the administrative work of this post to his deputy. That he did not let his duties lie too heavily upon him is indicated by the fact that after his inauguration at the Herrenhaus, he never put in another appearance.

Shortly after the completion of "Armida" Dvořák's health began to fail. He did not realize how serious his condition was — he had uremia and hardening of the arteries — and began making notes for a new opera. In the middle of April he got much worse but, when a slight improvement set in, was allowed by the doctor to take the midday meal with his family. One day he felt unwell, and was quickly brought back to his bed; he lost consciousness almost immediately, and the doctor, summoned in haste, pronounced him dead of a stroke. This was on May 1st, 1904.

Like Smetana, Dvořák lies buried in the graveyard of Vyšehrad. He was one of the last simple music-makers of the nineteenth century. His work shows two streams of influence: that of the classical masters, of Brahms, and to a slight extent of Wagner, and that exerted by the folk music of his native land. It is primarily his symphonies and chamber music which complement and continue the work of Smetana.